Comparative
Educational Systems

THE LIBRARY OF EDUCATION

A Project of The Center for Applied Research in Education, Inc.

G. R. Gottschalk, Director

Categories of Coverage

I	II	III
Curriculum and Teaching	Administration, Organization, and Finance	Psychology

IV	V	VI
History, Philosophy, and Social Foundations	Professional Skills	Educational Institutions

Comparative
Educational Systems

ARTHUR H. MOEHLMAN

Graduate Professor of the History
and Philosophy of Education
The University of Texas

1963
The Center for Applied Research in Education, Inc.
Washington, D.C.

LIBRARY OF CONGRESS
CATALOG CARD NO.: 63-13277

PRINTED IN THE UNITED STATES OF AMERICA

Foreword

To understand any system of education one must understand the people who created it: their land, history, and culture. Since such understanding is hard to achieve, complete, truthful, and perceptive descriptions of education in other lands are hard to find.

Why should anyone attempt to study comparative education? Why is the ability to understand and interpret another system of education an important skill? Through a sympathetic study of a foreign educational system, one gains a window through which the scholar may become acquainted with the national character and aspirations of another people. The next generation of man is being shaped by today's schools and colleges. The study of the motivation, the goals, and the techniques of a system of education is an important step toward understanding both this generation and the next. The achievement of such understanding is a firm step toward survival. *Comparative Educational Systems* provides a valuable reference and guide concerning this critical field of study for the scholar, student, and citizen.

The situation is complicated for our generation by massive and intense changes which are taking place throughout the community of man. These changes must be taken into consideration in judging educational developments. Education is in a state of flux because society is changing. A tide is sweeping against the barriers of group, race, creed, and nationality. Because of the revolution in transportation and communication, men and women almost everywhere are increasingly aware of their common humanity. The fantastic increase in human population in our times is another change which affects all of humanity. It is estimated that there were about 800 million people in 1800; by 1910 this number had doubled. The 1960 population was approximately double that of 1900, and by 2000 the population may double again.

The "revolution in expectations" has become paramount. Until recently the underprivileged were generally content to blame fate for their misfortunes and accepted them with resignation. But the lowly and the meek have developed new expectations. They are no longer content to be hungry and ignorant. They demand a better future for their children. Today's underprivileged generally believe there is a direct relationship between ignorance and hunger. They regard education as the door to a better life. They demand equal access, through education, to the good things of life.

One of the most dangerous phenomena of our times is the shift in the world power structure. Those who were first have lost some of their prestige, and those who were last have joined the councils of the world. The rising tide of independence in Africa and Asia has created many tensions which require for their solution vast knowledge, wisdom, and courage.

More than a third of mankind lives in Communist countries. It is difficult to overestimate the danger to the non-Communist world which is inherent in Communist ideology. This struggle will be settled on the basis of the relative power of the Communist and capitalist masses, regardless of whether the issue is settled by war or by peaceful competition. Education is a primary key to the future because education is the foundation of the intelligence and effectiveness of mass power, whether Communist or capitalist.

Another change which is affecting history is the sudden expansion of knowledge. Until recently education sometimes could remain static because the body of important knowledge available to each succeeding generation remained fundamentally static. Nowadays the mass of facts in any important area of learning grows overnight and whole new sciences have emerged. Education today is forced to pick and choose, to establish priorities, and sometimes to teach subjects unknown a generation ago.

The sudden emergence of great new frontiers produces major impacts upon educational development. Some of these frontiers are scientific, such as the growth of cybernetics, electronics, and the various operations associated with nuclear energy. Some are related to the changes in the development of human potentialities which are enormous. Other frontiers which are spatial are just now beginning to be appreciated. These frontiers are the equatorial jungles, the empty deserts, the potential treasures of Antarctica, and the water areas of the earth's surface, particularly the wealth of the oceans. Man's most fabulous adventures may await him in outer space.

These dynamic movements are effecting substantial changes in education. The nature of the new education developing during this time of transition depends on the action of the forces previously described upon traditional educational trends, of which the following have special significance. Nationalism has always been a dominant trend with many aspects, some good, some destructive, and is a powerful force in all countries. Education is used to instill national pride in the past and to form a bulwark of national loyalty and unity.

Elitism is another notable aspect of education. Elite education is the foundation of class distinction. In many societies all children follow a common curriculum to the age of eleven or twelve, then an examination separates the mass from the elite. The young elite receive the best and broadest education available. Their less fortunate brothers and sisters undertake a shorter terminal course with a strong vocational content. It is increasingly clear that it is impossible to assess accurately the potentialities of the human mind at eleven, or at any other specific time in the life of a child.

It is evident that trained intelligence is the foundation of power in the modern state, and that no state can afford to waste its talents. Therefore, democratic universal education has grown rapidly in the twentieth century. The democratic idea that adequate education is the right of every competent child is probably becoming the dominant educational philosophy of our world. Every child is supposed to have an equal chance to rise to the top. Arguments about relative standards in American and European schools, especially at the secondary level, are really directed at the comparative strengths of elite and democratic education.

Functionalism and classicism are basic trends in education. Functionalism is a belief that education should serve specific functions of value to society. Abroad, it is regarded as a peculiarly American concept which is being adapted to the needs of other cultures. The Soviet educational system is functional in that it is built on the idea that the minds of the young are the chief resource of the Socialist State, that a chief responsibility of the State is to enable each mind to make its maximum contribution to the collective welfare.

Classicism is in many ways the antithesis of functionalism. Classical education teaches the ideas and language of the past both to preserve the memory of things past and also because the ideas and languages of the past are thought to have special merit as the basic cultural heritage. It is easy to criticize classicism, but its faults are the faults of excess. A balanced knowledge of the past is necessary to understand the present. The past truly is prologue. It is paradox that a balanced classicism is in the best sense functional. In an ideal society there could be no contest between classicism and functionalism.

The pressures described earlier are having a powerful effect on the trends in the development of education everywhere. There is a strong tendency toward democracy as opposed to elitism. Countries are increasingly educating on the principle that the minds of its children are the greatest single resource of the state. The curriculum is becoming universal, as opposed to national. Whereas nations in one cultural tradition in the past have trained their children almost exclusively within that tradition, there is now an increasing understanding that education must deal with man as a family if the human race is to survive.

There is a strong tendency today to exalt the role of science. This grows from many roots. There is also a considerable interest in the pragmatic applications of science to the solution of human problems, especially in the developing countries. Fortunately, there is also evidence of a humanistic revival. It would be sad indeed if man lost his soul in a race to achieve power through science. But the new nations, as well as the old, take pride in their cultural traditions and perpetuate these traditions through education. All in all, there seems to be a world-wide awakening of interest in the arts. This is reflected in the content of education. The schools may be leading the way to a renaissance of humanism. Education is becoming more pragmatic, or more functional. This trend is in part a result of the need to use education as a social and political tool. It also is a natural result of the profusion and proliferation of modern knowledge. There is a new priority on the identification and training of the talented, and on the improvement of guidance services. There is great interest in developing improved teaching devices and techniques, and in improving the general competence of the teacher.

There is an active but uneven reaction to the rising educational pressures around the world. In some countries education has become the chief policy instrument of the government, and expenditures for education exceed all other public investments. But in some countries, there is a severe split between those who believe that advanced education should be reserved for the elite, and those who believe the national interest requires that all children be fully educated. It is possible that the rapid decline in power and prestige of some nations is, at least in part, a direct result of their failure to make appropriate use of education as a means of developing their human resources and potentialities.

How does one evaluate educational developments in another culture? Since each system of education is part of the warp and woof of its own culture, it is dangerous to generalize concerning any system of education without an exhaustive understanding of its culture. No segment of any culture can be understood save in relation to the whole. Scholars who know only education are handicapped in evaluating foreign systems of education. Scholars must use a critical morphology while exploring an educational system.

The successful scholar of comparative education should cultivate a capacity for creative intuition. Language, distance, and cultural differences all are obstacles to effective understanding. Great scholars seem to be able to transcend such obstacles and arrive at an approximation of the truth. This ability is marked by charity and humility. Arrogance and intolerance are permanent barriers to the clarity of understanding.

Professor Moehlman has outstanding qualifications for writing in the field of comparative education. He has been trained both in the United States and abroad in education, the humanities, and the social sciences at the University of Rochester and the University of Basel. His M. A. and Ph. D degrees were taken in history and the social sciences together with a certificate in education at the University of Michigan. He has carried out field surveys of education in Europe, Asia, Africa, and the Americas. His teaching experience includes the Universities of Michigan, Ohio State, Iowa, and Texas. He has held summer lectureships at the Universities of Rochester, Maine, and Stanford. During World War II he rose through the ranks from lieutenant to colonel in the U. S. Army General Staff and served with missions abroad in the European, African, and Asiatic areas. During residence as a Fulbright Research Professor at the University of Paris he completed the volume *Comparative Education*. Dr. Moehlman has conducted research in comparative education with colleagues and graduate students from the United States and abroad. He has worked with UNESCO, Ministries of Education in various countries, and with the Bureau of International Education of the United States Office of Education. Dr. Moehlman has produced a significant contribution to international scholarship in his *Comparative Educational Systems*.

OLIVER J. CALDWELL

Contents

CONTENTS

CHAPTER I

Introduction to
Comparative Educational Systems

This monograph is designed to explore certain basic questions essential to the understanding of systems of education as instruments of national policy. The questions may be phrased as follows: What are the major long-range factors which shape the primary components and characteristics of all educational systems? How do these factors influence the pattern of growth of educational systems in various cultures? What are the main trends in the development of educational systems? How effective are educational systems in coping with paramount issues in the survival of human culture?

In the pursuit of these questions we can investigate the significance of the role of education in human civilization. As we improve our methods of inquiry and investigation, we can illuminate the strengths and weaknesses of systems of education in various cultures.

Pioneers in the field of comparative education—I. L. Kandel, Friedrich Schneider, Pedro Rossello, Harold Benjamin, Leo Fernig, Oliver Caldwell, and many others—have phrased these basic questions and led the way in exploring them. As they foresaw, studies of comparative educational systems required the cooperation of specialists in comparative education and a wide range of experts from the various related disciplines such as philosophy, history, economics, sociology, geography, statistics, linguistics, psychology, law, and medicine.

Chapter I describes the major factors determining the primary characteristics of educational systems and the problems of formulating a cultural morphology essential for comparative studies of the main educational trends emerging within each system. Chapters II, III, IV, and V deal with case studies of the impact of these long-range factors in various cultures upon specific educational systems and with the significant characteristics developed in the process. Chapter VI investigates the main trends in educational development

1

with regard to orientation, organization, and operation. Chapter VII examines paramount issues facing all educational systems under the impact of long-range factors affecting their pattern of educational growth and which must be coped with effectively.

The approach in this monograph unites both the investigation of educational systems developing in the context of individual cultures and the analysis of the major problems of educational systems as topics or criteria. Experts in anthropology, psychology, law, government, and history have found it essential in their comparative studies to analyze the indigenous growth of universal activities or institutions within a culture and also to analyze a specific universal such as education and its major aspects topically in different cultures. The investigator as an academic scholar, government official, or general citizen needs to use both the comparative study of education's evolution in various cultures and of major trends in education's major components appearing in different nations. He is inevitably concerned with the patterns or forms of similarity and contrast which are the basis of comparative studies. He cannot afford to be provincial, naïve, or fanatic. Education is so deeply imbedded in the total pattern of its indigenous culture that it requires the use of both methods of inquiry—cultural and topical. Theoretical isolation of education can create artificial, misleading views of its form and reality.

As we move into humanity's vast future, there are new frontiers for comparative studies of educational systems requiring steadily increasing cooperation and interchange between specialists in comparative education and experts in other basic disciplines. Gardner Murphy, the psychologist, has pointed out that we must advance the enrichment of our human potentialities in a time marked by rapid acceleration in mechanical and physical potentialities. Dean Rusk, while president of the Rockefeller Foundation, underlined the fundamental importance of appreciating every nation's pride in its own indigenous culture as a basic factor in international relationships. Edward T. Hall, the anthropologist, has outlined a map of culture in which international differences and similarities can be analyzed by scholars and government officials on the basis of primary message systems dealing with learning, space, time, and other universal long-range factors in various cultures.

The needs and opportunities in comparative study of educational systems are rich and extensive if we remember the fundamental significance of the human power of wandering and diversification. As Alfred North Whitehead put it:

> When man ceases to wander, he will cease to ascend in the scale of being. Physical wandering is still important, but greater still is the power of man's spiritual adventures—adventures of thought, adventures of passionate feeling, adventures of aesthetic experience. A diversification among human communities is essential for the provision of the incentive and material for the Odyssey of the human spirit.[1]

Democracy demands diversity; dictatorship, uniformity. Democracy requires universal education with equal opportunity for everyone to learn the wide spectrum of truth concerning themselves and the universe, rather than the narrow spectrum permitted by any totalitarianism with its questionable assumptions of historical inevitability. Albert Einstein was thinking of these things and elitism when he wrote, "Restricting the body of knowledge to a small group deadens the philosophical spirit of a people and leads to spiritual poverty." He was keenly aware of the dangers to the great body of human knowledge in totalitarian education with its trends toward *suppressio veri et suggestio falsi*.

All systems of education have values. Intelligent comparative studies of educational systems can advance international understanding, world peace, and mutual aid so essential against humanity's perennial and implacable enemies: disease, drought, disaster, ignorance, and war.

Nations need to face the great issues of ethics and faith, aesthetics and utility, adventure and peace, freedom and discipline arising from the impact of such long-range factors as religion, art, philosophy, technology, and government. The viewpoints of scientific humanism and cultural relativism are of the essence if educational systems are to cope effectively with these paramount issues.

Definitions and Development

The study of comparative education can be justified by two quotations: "To know thyself, compare thyself to others" (Tacitus) and

---

[1] A. N. Whitehead, *Science and the Modern World* (New York: The Macmillan Company, 1925), p. 298.

"Those who forget their past are condemned to repeat it" (Santayana). This monograph on comparative educational systems is based upon these themes. One must devise and use a theoretical model for systematic comparative analysis investigating both contemporary trends in educational patterns and the impact of long-range factors: ethical, aesthetic, scientific, technological, social, political, and economic which shape educational systems in historical perspective. Studies of the contemporary patterns of education are essential but they must avoid a naïve empiricism which overlooks the continuity of civilization and its search for values essential to its own survival and progress.

Education may be defined as a lifelong social process of directed learning which enables both the individual and society to use the past's treasure of cultural inheritance, to operate effectively the institutions of the present, and to plan and invent wisely for the future. Today, youth must be educated for the unpredictable conditions which the future will bring. Barbara Ward, in her essay "A New Economic Strategy," insisted that the democracies of the Western world must recognize that they live in a world of revolution. She declared that we face

> ... a world of violence, catastrophe, and deepening revolution, and one in which whole societies will founder if they try to rely simply on the sailing charts for calm weather. Only if this reality is accepted can the western powers push safely on through the hurricane. For hurricane it is. Let us first look at the scale of the contemporary revolution; perhaps it would be more accurate to speak of the five or six revolutions, all of which are going on simultaneously over the face of the earth. The scientific revolution, the industrial revolution, the technological revolution, the national and popular revolution— begun and now more or less controlled in the Atlantic areas—are violently at work everywhere else.[2]

These revolutions have been accelerated by education.

In defining education's role in civilization, we must recognize the conflict between maintaining the massive cultural inheritance from the past in a symbolic code and fearlessly facing the challenges of the present and future requiring its revision. Alfred North Whitehead put it this way:

---

[2] Barbara Ward, "A New Economic Strategy," *The Atlantic Monthly* (February, 1959), p. 57.

It is the first step in sociological wisdom to recognize that the major advances in civilization are processes which all but wreck the societies in which they occur:—like unto an arrow in the hand of a child. The art of free society consists first in the maintenance of the symbolic code; and secondly in fearlessness of revision, to secure that the code serves those purposes which satisfy an enlightened reason. Those societies which cannot combine reverence to their symbols with freedom of revision, must ultimately decay either from anarchy, or from the slow atrophy of a life stifled by useless shadows.[3]

Education, regarded as a totality, is not only a systematic unity, a discipline operating in the present, but also a historical unity. Professor Meyer-Abich, in his lectures on the "Historico-Philosophical Definition and Classification of Biology," suggested that "any science [branch of knowledge] represents a historical period and develops itself historically. ... Biology in its totality is not only a systematic unity but also a historical unity." He went on to point out that a science or area of knowledge, such as biology or education, is a systematic unity or classification valid for its own period or epoch—each of which is derived from the past and opens up new aspects for the future.

Therefore, if we wish to undertake comparative studies in education we must have a theoretical model—a law of form or a morphology which enables us to examine education in its cultural structure not only as a contemporary systematic unity but also as an evolving historical unity. Each culture has its own indigenous process of educational growth but cultures must be studied comparatively for their reactions to the impacts of long-range environmental factors.

Kandel, in his *Comparative Education,* asked the basic question: "What are the factors which determine the character of an educational system?" In his original classic volume, *Triebkräfte der Pädagogik der Völker,* Friedrich Schneider presented his own significant exposition of the formative factors in the educational systems of all cultures: folk character; geographical space (natural environment); culture and civilization (cultural environment); social class struc-

---

[3] A. N. Whitehead, *Symbolism* (New York: The Macmillan Company, 1958), p. 88.

ture; historical development and destiny; politics; influence of foreign areas; internal evolution of educational ideas.[4]

He included science (or knowledge), philosophy, economics, and religion as extensions of the cultural environment. Schneider emphasized the influence of the foreign area and culture contacts as a formative factor—*i.e.*, the process of acculturation—and also underlined the spontaneous evolution of education in and of itself without external stimuli. His recent book *Vergleichende Erziehungswissenschaft* (1961) reinforces this approach to the comparative science of education. Influenced by Eduard Spranger's writing on the morphology of culture, Schneider believes with Compayre that *"Tout système philosophique contient en germe une pédagogie spéciale."*

Comparative Morphology

How may we study the role of education in civilization as the universal which enables all the other human activities or institutions to operate? What are the factors to be placed in the morphology? What are the variables which embody the human reaction to the opportunities or dangers presented by the cultural environment?

The following examples of culture morphologies illustrate various ways of describing the universal long-range factors in cultures which human beings develop to face the challenge of living.

Melville J. Herskovits summarized the universal aspects of culture in the following progression:

Material culture and its sanctions
  Technology
  Economics

Social institutions
  Social organizations
  Education
  Political structures

Man and the universe
  Belief systems
  The control of power

---

4 Friedrich Schneider, *Triebkräfte der Pädagogik der Völker, Eine, Einfuhrung in die Vergleichende Erziehungswissenschaft* (Salzburg: Otto Müller Verlag, 1947), p. 39.

Aesthetics
> Graphic and plastic arts
> Folklore
> Music, drama and the dance

Language[5]

He assumed a spatial and temporal setting for any grouping of physical types and assigned education a role as a universal long-range factor equal in rank to technology and political structure.

Edward T. Hall, in *The Silent Language,* has described operational criteria for universal activities or long-range factors applicable to culture systems for comparative purposes:

> These criteria are operational. That is, they are based on direct observation of the actual functioning of a cultural system, in this case, language. The criteria, from an anthropological point of view, are firm. There are ten separate kinds of human activity which I have labeled Primary Message Systems (PMS). Only the first PMS involves language. All the other PMS are nonlinguistic forms of the communication process. Since each is enmeshed in the others, one can start the study of culture with any one of the ten and eventually come out with a complete picture. The Primary Message Systems (in Hall's morphology) are:

> 1. Interaction—(language and communication)
> 2. Association—(government and politics)
> 3. Subsistence—(economics and consumption)
> 4. Bisexuality—(family and social structure)
> 5. Territoriality—(space and geography)
> 6. Temporality—(time and history)
> 7. Learning—(education and schools)
> 8. Play—(arts and recreation)
> 9. Defense—(religion and health)
> 10. Exploitation—(technology and science)[6]

Hall has produced an invaluable cultural morphology which is related in his general analysis of formal, informal, and technical aspects of human activities to terms describing universal human activities generally used, which are indicated in the parentheses above. As can be seen, Hall included time and space in his morphol-

---

[5] Melville J. Herskovits, *Man and His Works* (New York: Alfred A. Knopf, 1949), p. 239.
[6] Edward T. Hall, *The Silent Language* (Garden City, N. Y.: Doubleday & Company, Inc., 1959), pp. 61ff.

ogy but not physical types. The preceding survey of various approaches to comparative morphology underlines the difficulty and importance of selecting a balanced list of universal activities or long-range factors.

A comparative approach to the process of educational growth may enable us not only to make an analysis of the capabilities of a system of education but also to formulate more reliable relative trend analyses on the basis of a more valid theoretical model or morphology embodying long-range factors. For example, the original National Defense Education Act of the United States at one time based its policy and operation upon an educational trend analysis which required concentration upon acceleration of science, mathematics, foreign languages, and guidance with related research. This estimate did not sufficiently take into account the need for development of human potentialities through other channels—namely, philosophy, history, health education, and so on, and was too narrowly focused in its approach. Let us turn to the problem of selection of long-range factors essential to a morphology adequate for systematic comparative analysis.

Long-Range Factors

A primary problem in the formulation of a theoretical model or morphology is therefore the selection and depiction of the long-range factors which determine a system of education's orientation, organization, and operation—*i.e.,* effectiveness—in a culture or nation. Then the model may be applied comparatively to various systems of education. An adequate model should introduce long-range factors into the current trend analysis of educational systems. These long-range factors are variables which constitute human responses to challenges in the environment, both as obstacles and opportunities. Such factors form links between the professional discipline of education and other basic disciplines.

This approach should stimulate the student of education to ask certain basic questions with the aid of colleagues from other disciplines while concentrating upon the analysis of specific educational problems which are both contemporary and historical. Furthermore, these long-range factors can also provide non-educational analysts interested in education an opportunity to use their disciplines with their data and methods of inquiry for general analysis of the phenomena of the process of educational growth. Such an emphasis upon links between methods of inquiry in education and other disciplines can produce more useful professional exchanges in the comparative study of education.

A possible theoretical model for analysis of human educational response to challenges in its context of time, space, and culture includes the following long-range factors:

Folk—Ethnic sources, quantity, quality, and age structure of population.
Space—Spatial concepts, territoriality, and natural features.
Time—Temporal concepts, historical development, and evolution of culture.
Language—Symbols, message systems, and communication of conceptual thought.
Art—Aesthetics, search for beauty and play.
Philosophy—Value choices, pursuit of wisdom and the good life.
Religion—Relation of man and the universe, belief systems.
Social structure—Family, kinship, sex, etiquette, and social classes.
Government—Ordering of human relations, governmental structures and operations.
Economics—Satisfaction of wants, exchange, production, and consumption.
Technology—Use of natural resources through machines, techniques, and power resources.
Science—The sphere of knowledge concerning both natural and human realms.
Health—The condition of physical, mental, and emotional well-being, including functions of living.
Education—The social process of directed learning, both formal and informal.

These factors may be visualized as a "circle of humanity" in a space-time continuum, constantly in a process of acculturation.

The impact of these long-range factors determines the profile of education. With these factors, we can evaluate the wisdom and adequacy of a system of education's responses to major challenges. The factors have integral ratios of growth and decline which interact upon each other and determine the efficiency of education. Conversely, the integral characteristics of change in the educational pattern have marked effects upon the environment of the other long-range factors in which it exists. Each factor should be studied in its parent discipline.

The concept of time and history, for example, has been a basic factor in all cultures. Bernard Bailyn, in his *Education in the Forming of American Society*, wisely insisted upon a "broader definition of education and a different notion of historical relevance" in order to understand the first and fundamental change in American education completed before the close of the colonial period. This transformation, in Bailyn's well-chosen words:

> ... becomes apparent when one thinks of education not only as formal pedagogy but as the entire process by which a culture transmits itself across the generations; ... when one sees education in its elaborate involvements with the rest of society, and notes its shifting functions, meanings and purposes ... and it becomes evident also when one assumes that the past was not incidentally but essentialy different from the present.

Bailyn underlined the fact that education, or the social process of directed learning, is both a mirror and a catalyst: "education not only reflects and adjusts to society; once formed, it turns back upon it and acts upon it." In the colonial period, American education was transformed: First it became an instrument of radical social change, "a powerful internal accelerator" which released the energies of individuals and groups, and gave the young a lead time in new ideas gained from the immediate educational environment away from the control of family elders. Second, American education played a major role in shaping the national character and personality, individualistic, independent, and frontier-like.[7]

The environment's impact upon a system of education is transformed as the instruments devised to control it increase in power and sophistication. Our concept of the environment is sometimes called our *Weltbild* or world picture. As Lucien Febure pointed out in his admirable book *A Geographical Introduction to History,* in the past we may have overemphasized the direct effect of landscape, wind, sun and rain, plants and animals upon a particular human culture. Cultures of Britain and Japan, for instance, have pursued quite different paths despite the fact that both developed on islands on the rim of the Eurasian continent and at the edge of great oceans.

---

[7] Bernard Bailyn, *Education in the Forming of American Society* (Chapel Hill, N.C.: University of North Carolina Press, 1960), pp. 14, 48.

Our historical attitudes toward our surrounding landscape and environment have changed. In the past the landscape has been viewed as an ever-present natural resource to be fully exploited and also as a hostile force against which the struggle for existence and survival of the fittest was waged. Paul Sears in his *Deserts on the March* points to the deforestation of large portions of the earth's landscape—including the Mediterranean lands, China, and areas of North America—as an example of this destructive trend. Now, the development of a different view of environment has been found to be essential. Any organisms which destroy their environment eventually destroy themselves; those organisms survive which cooperate in creatively modifying their environment for their mutual benefit.

Patterns of Educational Analysis

A pattern of education constitutes a complex organism which is always difficult to analyze. In over a quarter century's experience, Dr. Pedro Rossello, Assistant Director of the International Bureau of Education, has created a logical and practical series of categories for comparative study of developmental trends in various cultures. As he said in *The XXI International Yearbook of Education* (1959), his "Comparative Study of Educational Progress" has—year by year—both given a "silhouette of educational advance" and suggested "the rhythm of development." He would like to have more precise instruments for measurement of trends, but, as he says, "The constancy of the results obtained over successive years is nevertheless reassuring and leads us to believe that when complete data are available the results will not differ in their broad outlines from those at present obtained by approximate methods." Dr. Rossello has made some valuable vertical comparisons of the evolution of education in each given country. He agrees with fellow researchers that the degree of importance in major aspects of educational development is very difficult to evaluate in numerical form.[8]

His pattern of educational analysis includes the following primary categories for analysis of trends: administration, free compulsory education, primary education, secondary education, vocational education, higher education, and teaching staff. The policy for orienta-

---

[8] Pedro Rossello, *The International Yearbook of Education* (Geneva: International Bureau of Education and UNESCO, 1959), pp. 11, 12.

tion and strategy in a nation's education stands out clearly when analyzed under these categories. A category for general philosophy of education could be added, for, although philosophy cannot be statistically structured, it can be delineated as a value system and related to the more quantitative categories.

UNESCO has made many valuable contributions to the comparative study of educational systems, especially with regard to patterns of analysis for developmental trends. These are set forth in *World Handbook of Educational Organization and Statistics* (Paris, 1952); *World Survey of Education* (Paris, 1955); *World Survey of Education, II, Primary Education* (Paris, 1958); *World Survey of Education, III, Secondary Education* (Paris, 1961). All of the volumes possess excellent chapters on the basic problems of comparative exposition and statistical reporting of educational systems as well as the reports on separate national systems of education and glossaries of school terms.

Leo Fernig, Peter Wells, and other members of the UNESCO staff have shown great intellectual ingenuity in devising solutions for problems of comparative description in the historical surveys, the Fork Diagrams showing flow of stages of education and types of institutions, and the Statistical Diagrams depicting the percentages of population attending educational establishments. One of the most useful analyses is Chapter II of *World Survey of Education* (Paris, 1955), an excellent critique of the work of comparative educationists.

Strategies of Education and National Style

An educational system possesses a strategy reflecting and supporting the national style. The concept of national style concerns itself with the general plan of attack used by a nation or civilization to solve its major problems. W. W. Rostow's *The United States in the World Arena* is a valuable interpretation of American national style and its possible destiny. A strategy of education must continually strive to evolve a national style which can cope with a rapidly changing environment.

An educational system must provide firm steps toward national survival. In writing this comparative analysis of educational systems, I have thought of my teacher, Dexter Perkins, and of his rule of thumb as expressed in his *Popular Government and Foreign Policy:*

> The Abbé Siéyès, that ingenious and flexible Frenchman of the period of the French Revolution, was once asked what he had done during those stirring years of convulsion. "I have survived" was his reply. Precisely so. The first test of a regime is its capacity to perpetuate itself.[9]

The United States and other democracies have survived thus far but there is no guarantee that they will continue to survive.

Cultures must have a strategy of education which builds up the national style's ability to meet new challenges of immediate disaster or insidious decline. Systematic comparative study of education in relation to other long-range factors in human development can help us to obtain a sharper picture of our successes and failures in educational strategy and national style. A team approach is essential: comparative education specialists need the aid of other experts in the discipline of education—above all, historians and philosophers of education whose methods of inquiry contribute depth and insight to comparative educational research. The specialists in curriculum and methods, instructional materials, evaluation and measurements, administration, and educational psychology are basic consultants in systematic comparative research. (See *Philosophy of Education,* by Professor Burns, *History of Education* by Professor Medlin, and those by other specialists in this series.) Comparative education needs to exploit links with the other disciplines whose bodies of knowledge and methods of inquiry encompass the other long-range factors in civilization. The anthropologists, geographers, historians, philosophers, economists, sociologists, political scientists, and linguists in the *Geisteswissenshaften* have contributed and will contribute new dimensions to the discipline of education as a comprehensive transmission of civilization.

The analysis of an educational system in its culture context involves comparison with the investigator's own national pattern of education and with other nations. Studies of foreign educational systems as historical and systematic unities are not limited to description but include comparative analysis. One of the great rewards

---

[9] Dexter Perkins, *Popular Government and Foreign Policy* (New York: Fund for Adult Education, 1956), p. 10.

of comparative educational study is the fascinating exploration of education's patterns in various cultures. No one can predict which educational strategies will serve the human race best in its further conquest of freedom.

Various countries in the European, Asian, African, and American culture areas present valuable examples of educational strategies from which all may learn. The world needs educational pluralism and constructive acculturation. Diversity in human civilizations helps inculcate the elements of humility and modesty which the Greeks called *aidos*, basic in man's search for the truth. If there is no check upon pride and arrogance (*hubris*), men move toward a paramount danger of our times: a cosmic insolence arising from their intoxication with personal and social power.

CHAPTER II

Education in European Culture Areas

Europe has developed a rich diversity in education and civilization which has been and is a catalyst for the entire world. Each of the European culture areas has contributed greatly to the advancement of knowledge and human happiness. They have expanded across the oceans and have penetrated all the continents. Europe began the modern revolution in education: she invented the modern university as a center of research and teaching, the secondary grammar schools, the universal elementary schools, and the kindergartens. Each culture area created its own indigenous pattern of education. Four different educational systems have been selected for analysis: English, French, German, and Russian.

England

England's physical detachment from the continent of Europe permitted the development of a unique culture which is mirrored in its education. (An index to the English frame of mind is provided by the news headline *"STORM RAGES IN CHANNEL. CONTINENT ISOLATED."*) How did various long-range factors shape the English pattern of education? What are the main characteristics of this pattern and how well can it cope with paramount issues that challenge all educational systems? How do certain contemporary Englishmen, such as C. P. Snow, Geoffrey Crowther, and M. V. C. Jeffreys estimate the situation of their educational system?

Certain long-range factors have molded the English educational system. The English people are a mixed race of various invading stocks, Iberian originally, then Celtic and Roman, Anglo-Saxon and Norman French. As the historian Trevelyan pointed out, before 1066 England was easy to invade from the low eastern and southern shores. The rugged mountains of Wales, Cornwall and Scotland provided refuge for the older Iberian, Celtic, and other stocks successively. Her social structure was made up of a Saxon-speaking population ruled by Norman French-speaking overlords and a Latin-speaking clergy. On this island, no point of which is more than seventy miles from the sea, an indigenous civilization grew up strong enough to prevent further invasions and to build a base for its own expansion. The language was an amalgam of Celtic, Latin, Teutonic, and French. It became increasingly flexible and concise, with few inflections and a rich vocabulary.

This new English-speaking culture was ruled by an elite which based its position on the possession of land. This elite shaped the direction of such long-range factors as economics, technology, politics, philosophy, religion, as well as social structure. In William of Wykeham's phrase, "Manners makeyth the man"; and the manners were those of an English gentleman: landowner, Anglican, and "gentry."

"County" society had its beginnings in the feudalism of the Middle Ages when the basic payment for all services was in land, and the common law revolved around land. In the sixteenth century, when feudalism was disappearing, Protestantism (in the form of the newly created Anglican Church) conveniently came on stage. The State confiscated the old Catholic Church estates which were sold or given to new owners. These new owners set the pattern for the succeeding centuries. They joined the landed aristocracy and emulated their feudal forerunners. Men rose socially through various forms of wealth, but they followed the pattern of buying landed estates to confirm their social position and to provide for political advancement. They imitated the manners, education, pastimes, and land management methods of the county society, whether they were seventeenth-century merchant adventurers, eighteenth-century "nabobs" from India, or nineteenth-century industrialists. The possession of land and its management, in this case, produced a ruling society which was open to men of talent and which fostered a sense of social responsibility or *noblesse oblige.*

The men of property were Anglican, and after the Puritan-Cavalier Civil War were able to restore the privileged position of the Established Church. Membership in the Anglican Communion was the key to proper education in the great "public" schools and the universities (*i.e.,* Oxford and Cambridge), and to careers in civil offices, the armed forces and politics.

The English system of residential Latin grammar schools and

the ancient colleges at Oxford and Cambridge did produce a century of genius—the seventeenth—with Coke (the Common Law), Newton (mathematics and physics), Boyle (chemistry), and Harvey (medicine). But in the nineteenth century the impact of the Industrial Revolution and urbanization exposed the shortcomings of the educational system. The Education Law of 1870 established free elementary or board schools to improve literacy and to meet the humanitarian and scientific demands of the elder Huxley and others that the schools should provide a ladder from the gutter to the highest places in the land. Only in 1902 did England obtain a secondary educational system open to all on a merit basis. The chief administrator of the authorizing act modeled the excellent new free grammar schools closely after his own "public school" *Weltanschaung* with stiff academic courses, plenty of sports, and training in ethical character. (Kipling caught the pattern of residential and day grammar schools in his short story "The Brushwood Boy.") The Fisher Act of 1917 moved English education further toward democratization. Finally, the Education Act of 1944 provided for the education of all children of secondary school age throughout England and Wales.

The pattern of the English educational system is diverse, reflecting the strata of its cultural history. The six-year primary school begins at five years of age and ends with the still highly selective "11-plus examination" which divides the candidates into three major secondary school groups: grammar, technical, and modern. This system has recently come under considerable criticism. The comprehensive school, which includes all three secondary curricula, has been added (it was originally a political objective of the Labor Party). In all English schools, pupils are "streamed" or grouped according to ability, with specialization in the upper two forms— that is, for sixteen–eighteen-year-olds.

The English universities are all independent, privately endowed, and financed by public funds which are apportioned by a unique body, the University Grants Committee, made up of members from the university faculties. The government does not control higher education and there are no state universities. Oxford and Cambridge still have the greatest prestige and emphasize the valuable and expensive tutorial system in individual residential colleges linked with general university lectures, amateur sports, musical groups, and debating organizations. The University of London has some features of the European universities. Universities usually require three years or more of study for medical degrees. Research is heavily emphasized and the specialization introduced in the last forms of the secondary schools is carried still further.

As Sir Percy Nunn pointed out in his very influential book, *Education, its Data and First Principles,* the English agree perhaps upon only one point in their educational philosophy—that the individual personality must be nurtured. Some eminent analysts applaud the high standards of English education, but Alfred North Whitehead said:

> My own criticism of our traditional educational methods is that they are far too much occupied with intellectual analysis and with the acquirement of formularized information. . . . We are too exclusively bookish in our scholastic routine. The general training should aim at eliciting our concrete apprehensions and should satisfy the itch of youth to be doing something.[1]

Professor M. V. C. Jeffreys, in his significant analysis of education *Glaucon,* argued for a more balanced liberal education. Geoffrey Crowther and his committee in their important report *15 to 18* recommended the continuation of early specialization with certain improvements. Sir C. P. Snow, in his unique analysis *Two Cultures and the Scientific Revolution,* pointed out the dangers of stressing early specialization and the training of an elite not large enough to cope with a new technology instead of changing to a broader system of studies and breaking through the universities' influence on secondary school syllabi through their control of the external examinations for the General Certificate of Education (at sixteen) and the Advanced Level G. C. E. (at eighteen). Snow called for a drastic rethinking of education so as to unite the traditional "literary" culture with the new "technological" culture.

There is much to be learned from detailed study of the growing impact upon English education of the Acts of 1902, 1913, and 1944 together with the laws setting up socialized health, welfare, and family support. The English have provided for increased equality of opportunity for the talented, and that elusive ruling elite, "the Establishment," now absorbs talent into its ranks from all classes,

---

[1] A. N. Whitehead, *Science and the Modern World* (New York: The Macmillan Company, 1925), pp. 284ff.

including the "angry young men." England is not complacent about her educational strategy and national style. The Government White Paper, *Secondary Education for All: A New Drive* (1958), states the case for equal access in accordance with ability and aptitude, and the value of variety in education:

> It is entirely natural and right that every parent should wish his children to attend the school from which they will derive the greatest possible benefit; and the anxiety of parents over "11-plus" will be finally allayed only when every secondary school, no matter what its description, is able to provide a full secondary education for each of its pupils in accordance with his ability and aptitude. . . . The history of education in this country is, to a large extent, a series of local histories. Individual schools have grown up in response to, and have been shaped by, local needs. The result is a considerable variety in the schools themselves and in the local schemes of organization within which they work. This variety is a valuable foundation on which to build for the future. The Government are convinced that this approach is best calculated to satisfy the needs both of the nation and of individual children.[2]

A senior education official in Britain discussed the shape of things to come in that country, and he finished on some such lines as this:

> We need more and better qualified teachers; we want to replace old school premises even more quickly than we have been achieving in the recent past; we want to ensure that every child whatever his ability, his social and economic background or his temperament is given the chance to fulfill himself to the very utmost that his talents and perseverance allow; we want to ensure that the curriculum of the schools is properly adapted to an industrial and scientific society; we want greatly to expand opportunities for higher education; and, above all, we want to make the rate-payers and tax-payers (on whom in the last resort all progress depends) realize that if we are to achieve all these things that are vital to a modern community, they have got to put their hands pretty deeply in their pockets.

The work of the Committee on Higher Education is only one evidence of the English moving to meet new challenges.

---

[2] Ministry of Education, *Secondary Education for All, A New Drive* (London: H. M. Stationary Office, 1958), p. 5.

France

France's culture and education represent a creative amalgam of the best of the Teutonic north and the Latin south. The French place primary emphasis upon the spiritually and intellectually complete individual, the *honnête homme,* who is regarded as the measure of all things and who can cope with all challenges through his education in a *culture générale.* The French schools stress the use of the individual's sensitivity and intellect as a means of measure and proportion in human living. They combat the fragmentation of the individual through early specialization. The French say *"il faut de tout pour faire un monde"*—a diversity of people is needed to make up the world.

Within France can be found every type of climate from the cool North Atlantic climate of Brittany's rocky peninsulas and sandy beaches to the Mediterranean climate of Languedoc and Provence on the south coast with the snow-capped Alps to the east. The more than forty-five million people of France are just as varied as their landscape, ranging from tall blond Normans to the stocky dark Latins. France, more than twice as large as Great Britain, has a variety of rich industries in heavily populated cities. About one-third of the population live on small mixed farms. They cultivate their land with real affection to produce fruit, cereals, wines, cheeses and dairy products and there are extensive fisheries along the sea.

French culture and education have produced great artists, such as Daumier, Cézanne, Monet, and Rodin; philosophers, such as Montaigne, Rousseau, and Bergson; and artists, writers, and playwrights, such as Molière, Victor Hugo, Balzac, and Rostand. The French have always been outstanding in the realm of technology and science. Lavoisier, Pasteur, and Becquerel are representative of the French contributors to science. There was the engineer Eiffel (about whom the French children still have a chant today *"La Tour Eiffel a trois cents metres"*), the architect Corbusier, and the inventor of modern reinforced concrete, Monier.

The French genius for leadership in world culture has had its major base in a unique educational development. The French strategy of education includes, first, the rapid extension of elementary education so that everyone is literate, can really think and has a basic comprehension of the complete life (*culture générale*); and second, a highly competitive secondary education so that the really talented have an opportunity to rise and to make full use of their abilities. How did the French evolve this effective strategy of education which has been attractive to many countries, from some sections of the United States to Turkey, Persia, Japan, and some of the developing countries of the twentieth century?

Social, economic, and other long-range factors have contributed to the development of France's unique education. In the beginning the Church and the religious orders made great contributions to the growth of education as did the revolutionary intellectuals or *philosophes* later on. By the thirteenth century, the University of Paris had developed from the cathedral schools. The great faculties of medicine, theology, law, the arts, and science were organized, and certificates were provided which permitted holders to teach and practice. The University of Paris not only fostered the faculties but also the significant scholastic philosophy brought to a peak under Thomas Aquinas. It formed the model for the modern university and was a primary intellectual invention giving Europe a scientific lead over the rest of the world. The University provided a realm for experimentation in teaching and learning which laid the groundwork for the modern French method of education. Such men as Abélard created the famous *sic et non* method of dialectic analysis for stating problems; the medieval teacher also used the *quod libet* method. The lecture method was perfected, giving a broad range of analysis and survey, and finally the *explication de texte,* in which a particular statement was analyzed from all sides. These methods of education, together with the insistence upon frequent writing of analytical papers, have been basic in the high standards reached by French education. The University of Paris was imitated throughout Europe and formed the basis for European pioneering in all areas of culture. At the same time the various religious orders were building up elementary and secondary schools, emphasizing not only the classical languages but also the very useful mathematics so important in the growing trade of the time.

In the sixteenth century Montaigne wrote his famous *Essays.* Many Frenchmen regard his essay on education as basic to any wise educational philosophy: *"la tête bien faite vaut mieux que la tête trop pleine"* (the well-trained mind is superior to a mind merely stuffed with facts). In the eighteenth century, the French Revolutionary leaders were convinced that clerical controls were basically hostile to the new republic. A great struggle began against any clerical control of education and politics. Condorcet wrote his splendid plan for universal education and the new republican government moved toward an elementary education which was *"gratuite, publique, laïque"* (free, public, and lay). Voltaire, too, fought against clerical control of education. Rousseau spoke for a new education, for the role of play, for close connection with nature, and —above all—for fostering the natural growth of the child rather than the training of children as miniature adults. Rousseau's writings on education influenced the entire world.

Before the Revolution the *philosophes* of the eighteenth century had taken the British idea of individual independence and converted it into a series of political proclamations, including the idea that education should be equally available to all men so that they could rise through ability rather than through family prestige or religious faith. In the nineteenth century Napoleon set the pattern for modern French education. He was a man of the people who had risen to supreme command through the competitive disciplined training of the army. Above all, he wanted a competently trained elite of leaders, administrators, and officers in civilian and military life. In 1808 he issued the decrees setting up the basic structure of French education. He concentrated upon advancement of the secondary school system and the university and in the main left elementary education to the clerical orders. As a good military man, he wished to make sure that all of his elite were equally well-trained by uniform methods under a strict discipline which selected and advanced students on the basis of merit. He set up the modern *lycées* which had a strict regime very similar to that of military barracks. Vestiges of that discipline persist to this day. Later on Daumier caricatured the "two by two," almost military outdoor walks of the *lycée* students.

The Franco-Prussian War convinced the French that they would have to improve their system of education as well as other aspects of their way of life. In 1881, after some controversy, one-sixth of the entire revenue of the Republic was alloted to public education. In this period both the elementary and secondary schools were improved in curriculum and methods. Laws were implemented to effect the separation of church and state in public education. Michelet, one of the greatest historians of the nineteenth century, made a wise and witty observation on education and government which is even more valid today: "What is a government's first task? Education. The second? Education. The third? Education."

The two-track system of universal elementary education and selective secondary and higher education continued to develop in France. The *départements,* or administrative subdivisions of France, were organized into sixteen educational regions or *académies,* each with a university whose *recteur* controlled all education from the university down to the elementary school, where the *département's* prefect took over. The prefect himself was still responsible through the *recteur* to the Minister of Education in Paris. Both clericals and anticlericals agreed that school was for the training of the mind and intellect. The French believed in a *culture générale* or general education based upon discipline of the intellect in the paramount ideas and books.

Pupils were selected for the *lycées* and the similar *collèges* at eleven, after five years of primary or elementary school. The *école communale,* or public school, included eight years of compulsory elementary education. In secondary education seven years of very hard work in the basic disciplines of classic and modern languages, science and mathematics, and history and social sciences led to the *baccalauréat* examinations. The *baccalauréat* was given by the university of the region in two sections as very difficult sets of external examinations. Successful completion of the *baccalauréat* permitted the student to go on to the universities or to the *grandes écoles.* French higher education was characterized by separation into the university with the traditional great faculties and the *Grandes Écoles* (advanced professional schools which are fully as difficult and carry as much prestige as the universities). The *Grandes Écoles* concentrate upon such professions as engineering, public administration, and education, while the universities emphasize the more traditional faculties. (In the United States we tended to combine the two.) The *École Polytechnique* for engineering and the *École Normale Supérieure* for advanced teacher education have acquired tremendous reputations. The French two-track system, aimed at producing a generally well-educated citizenry together with a competent professional elite, worked out very well and was imitated throughout the world; but certain difficulties and controversies became increasingly troublesome.

Too few rural, agricultural, and working-class students were going on into secondary and higher education. After World War I the French began to take definite steps to end the consequent loss of talent. It was clear that the selection of pupils for secondary schools at eleven years of age did not permit accurate judgments concerning their future abilities and careers: many children matured slower than others. Also, there was not sufficient attention given to needs for technological training and vocational education. The agitation for the *école unique,* or universal one-track system of education, got underway. Various committees, one of which was the Langevin Committee of 1946–47, made recommendations which moved toward bringing together the two-track system of education and allowing French youth to advance by paths other than that of the intellectual discipline. The Langevin recommendations of 1946–47 led the way to the setting up of *cours complementaires,* which permitted and encouraged able students to shift over from the *école communale* or eight-year public elementary school even after age eleven and to enter a *lycée* and move on through the university. In addition, there were set up *centres d'apprentissage,* which united training for the various crafts with a very good academic training.

The *Centre International des Études Pédagogiques* at Sèvres, under the able leadership of Edith Hatinguais and her colleagues, has pioneered in an advanced type of education, and is an experimental center for each level of education from the *Jardin des Enfants* through the elementary and the secondary grades and is co-educational throughout. Other experimental *lycées* are maintained at various points. In many sections of France, experiments were made in the *classes nouvelles* toward broadening the curriculum to include *étude du milieu,* the arts, and physical education. Provision was made for *orientation* or guidance, as suggested by Roger Gal and others, so that the students could choose the path best suited to them. With the decree of January, 1959, the period of compulsory education was extended from fourteen to sixteen years. By 1961 reforms in teaching included an observation and guidance, or orientation, stage for eleven- to thirteen-year-old students. The educational regions were increased to nineteen. In addition, the Lapie Committee recommended basic principles for reform including the integration of private schools into the state system.

Requirements for entrance into various kinds of secondary schools have undergone a change of emphasis: teachers' recommendations are now more important than external examinations. The *baccalauréat* system has been changed so that students specializing in certain scientific fields can take another, specialized, type of examination. There are still too few available openings in secondary and higher education, but the French have increased their education budget to provide for more.

The French strategy in education has been a successful one despite these difficulties. One of the significant testimonials to the success of the French system is that many new countries have used it for a model.

The French are able critics of their own system of education. They are fully aware of the disappointments experienced by many students in elite training. They know the educational difficulties involved in meeting the challenge of the generalized world of the mind as against the specialized world of technology, engineering, and the various applied sciences. The French are in a process of dynamic change which includes every one of the long-range factors in their culture from philosophy and religion to technology and social structure. Their educational system will be a primary instrument in their national struggle with the very difficult issues of the modern European Renaissance. The splendid volume, *L' explosion scolaire,* by Louis Cros presents a masterly exposition of the French appreciation of the schools' situation in the atomic age; the transformation of the structure, the adaptation of methods, and above all, the necessary effort. As Louis Cros says in closing: "De l'effort de formation des hommes, en effet, l'avenir dépend. Il faut que, chez nous comme ailleurs, cet effort prenne désormais la toute première place."[3]

Germany

Germany (*Das Reich der Mitte*) holds a strategic position between Eastern and Western Europe. It rises from the North Sea as part of the European plain, extending from England through Russia, into the *Mittelgebirge* and the higher Alps. The major rivers —the Rhine, the Weser, the Elbe, the Oder, and the Vistula—flow

---

[3] Louis Cros, *L'explosion scolaire* (Paris: CUIP, 1961), p. 178.

northwards while the Danube flows southeastward to the Black Sea. At the beginning of the 1960's, Germany had already lost territories east of the Oder-Neisse Line and was divided into the Federal Republic of Germany (approximately ninety-six thousand square miles and over fifty-five million people) and the German Democratic Republic (approximately forty-two thousand square miles and less than forty million people). A salient fact was that the old Germany had been divided into three parts: Western Germany between Rhine and Elbe, Middle Germany (now called The Zone) between Elbe and Oder, with German territory east of the Oder made into a part of Poland.

The Germans are a powerful people—industrious, indefatigable, and ingenious—who symbolize the struggle between force and freedom in human history and mirror it in their educational development. This is suggested by Jacob Burckhardt in his *Weltgeschichtliche Betrachtungen*.[4] This conflict is reflected in the contrast between German contributions to music, art, literature, philosophy, medicine, scientific research, and technology, and the German pursuit of national grandeur under a policy once called "blood and iron." The philosopher Kant, the authors Schiller and Goethe, the musicians Bach, Beethoven, and Brahms, and the scientists Robert Koch and Max Planck symbolize the German spirit of freedom; Bismarck, the Hohenzollerns, and Hitler, the spirit of force. German history has been a series of movements outward from the German lands since the third-century "Wandering of the Peoples" (*Völkerwanderung*), which affected the entire history of Western Europe. In the Middle Ages the Germans expanded eastward, as described in Thompson's *Medieval Germany,* moving down the Danube and eastward along the Baltic. The Hansa cities traded along the Northern Seas and German commerce moved over the mountains into the Mediterranean.

In the late Middle Ages the German school system began to take form. The universities followed the lead of the thirteenth-century University of Paris with the foundation of the great faculties of theology, law, the arts, and medicine. The Latin schools built up their prestige while Latin was the language of law, statecraft, and all intellectual pursuits. In the newly developing towns, both the

---

[4] J. Burckhardt, *Weltgeschichtliche Betrachtungen* (Basel: Füssli, 1929), pp. 24ff.

merchants and the artisans sent their children for at least a few years to the Latin schools as well as to the German burgher schools to learn reading and writing. Only later, in the sixteenth century, did the *Volkschule* (folkschool) begin to meet the needs of the churches of the Reformation and Counterreformation, absorbing the older German writing and reading schools of the towns. In the seventeenth century the German princes and states awakened to economic and worldly interests and encouraged the further advancement of schools and universities. In the eighteenth century the Germans began to make their outstanding contributions to education though many areas had not yet recovered from the devastations of the Thirty Years' War. The newly founded University of Göttingen formed the model of the new secular German university, demoting theology from its paramount position, emphasizing the pursuit of all organized scientific knowledge or *Wissenschaft,* and carrying on research and teaching at the same time. The three-way school system of Germany began to take its modern form. The educational system was divided into an eight-year *Volkschule* for all the working and artisan classes, followed by three years of education as an apprentice in the trades; the *Mittelschule* (middle school), designed for the middle classes who filled the ranks of lesser officials, business men, elementary school teachers, and so on; and the *Höhere Schulen* (higher schools)—i.e., the various *Gymnasia* which prepared students for the *Abitur* or final examinations required for entrance to the universities and were designed for the upper classes of higher officials, army officers, and all the professions. By the beginning of the nineteenth century the organization of this conservative school system designed for the maintenance of a class-structured society was already clear with a heavy weighting in the direction of the use of force and in conflict with the drive towards liberalism and freedom.

In the nineteenth century the conflict continued. The Germans fought against the French Revolution. Then the Revolution was carried into their land by Napoleon and although this was not Napoleon's intention the seeds of liberalism were sown by his armies. In the growth of national feeling stimulated by the Napoleonic occupation of Germany, the Prussians gradually took over leadership and their army and general staff became the symbol of German discipline and order (*Disziplin und Ordnung*). The almost militarily organized Prussian school system came into prominence. The Germans borrowed heavily from the great Swiss teacher Pestalozzi but they used his ideas to make their *Volkschule* more effective, not to turn the school into a delightful and creative family situation as Pestalozzi desired. The German elite reacted strongly against the contributions of their most liberal and creative educational personalities, such as Froebel's Kindergarten innovations and Herbart's advanced philosophy of teaching. Under the reactionary controls of Metternich and other statesmen, Germany swung so far to the right that after the failure of the Revolution of 1848 some of her best people emigrated to the New World where their educational ideas helped shape American educational development.

The Prussians played a large role in the structuring of German education by introducing the so-called *Reifeprüfung,* or test of readiness or competence. In 1834 Prussia insisted upon this state-administered external type of examination (the *Abitur*) as the prerequisite to matriculation into the university and the crucial state exams as a prerequisite for entrance into the bureaucracy and professions. Military service was decreased to a one-year volunteer period of service for those who completed the *Tertia* (the fourth year) in the *Gymnasium.* Economic and social developments produced pressure to add a separate middle school (*Mittelschule*) to follow the eight-year general *Volkschule* or elementary school. In 1872, the Prussian General Decrees set up specific curricula for the different kinds of higher schools (*Höhere Schulen*). In addition, the *Mittelschule* was characterized as an independent type of school with a general education which was to prepare for the middle-class callings. The trend was strongly toward three school types each delimited to its own social class and cultural level. Attendance at a particular school was really the affirmation of the social standing of the parents and the school was not an instrument for general development of all the talents of all the people. The liberal thinking of the nineteenth century in spiritual, social, and economic spheres began to modify this caste school system in the twentieth century.

The Germans gained in very definite ways from their stratified three-way school system. They trained an upper-class leadership elite, an excellent middle class of businessmen and minor officials, and an obedient lower class of well-trained workers, artisans, and farmers. One must also underline the accomplishments of the German drive toward complete literacy in the *Volkschule,* the general liberal education with much science and modern language in the *Gymnasia,* and the insistence upon a new educational approach which included the use of seminar and the laboratory in the universities. The major professors regarded their doctoral students as carefully selected intellectual apprentices who followed in their footsteps and extended their own well-organized work still further. The German universities were proud of their insistence upon freedom of teaching and freedom of learning (*Lehrfreiheit* and *Lernfreiheit*). Talented young men came from all over the world to study with these extraordinary German professors. To mention only a few, Ticknor, Everett and Cogswell studied at the University of Göttingen with its magnificent library and returned to pioneer in the teaching of Spanish literature, the introduction of the elective system, and the advancement of libraries.

Many persons believe that Horace Mann, the American educational pioneer in the mid-nineteenth century, put his finger upon the basic difficulty facing the Prussians and other Europeans: the students ended their eight-year elementary education at the age of fourteen, just when they were ready to make full use of their talents; only a few were selected to study further in the *Gymnasia* and an enormous amount of talent was wasted. Mann observed that there were no district school or town libraries in Prussia and that the newspapers were completely controlled by the government with no freedom of the press.

The rule by force in the highly efficient German educational system was shattered by World War I. The impact of military defeat and the subsequent economic depression prevented the liberal currents in postwar Germany from being as successful as they might have been. But in spite of many obstacles, the Weimar Republic did work out some very real advances in education and the old German tradition of pioneering in education continued. The *Einheitsschule,* or unified school, movement gained ground and resulted in a basic three-year and, later, four-year *Grundschule* or foundation school to which all children went. But the various reform movements which sought to provide more equal access to education for all were not able to make headway against the various reactionary trends. The most destructive trend came in the Nazi period, which combined the doctrine of force with a modern, technological, and scientific setting distorted by fanatical racial theories. The results for German education and for German culture in general were catastrophic. After the Nazis' seizure of power in 1933, National Socialism's hostility to the scientific search for truth blocked the development of the educational system. The number of students in German universities had been over 111,000 in 1929; it declined to approximately 56,000 in 1939. This regression not only struck at the *Geisteswissenschaften* (the humanities, literature, and social sciences), but also at the *Naturwissenschaften* (the natural sciences and many technological areas): in this same period the number of students majoring in chemistry declined from 4300 to 2900; the number of students majoring in engineering declined from 6700 to 3300.

At the close of World War II, Germany was in chaos with her major cities almost completely destroyed and only a few university towns and libraries untouched. Refugee children from Germany east of the Oder were pouring into West Germany. Social conditions were terrible and the outlook for educational reconstruction was very dark. With great difficulty the Germans and the occupying powers—the United States, Britain, France, and the Soviet Union, began to rebuild the educational system but in very different fashion east and west of the Elbe river. The American and British Zones gave as much responsibilty as possible to the Germans. The French kept somewhat closer control. The Russians took very rapid action installing a Soviet type of economy and school system. Soon the Eastern Zone people began to "vote with their feet" by escaping into West Berlin. This escape hatch, however, was closed by the building of the wall dividing the eastern and western sectors (August 13th, 1961).

West Germany not only produced a *Wirtschaftswunder* (economic miracle) but also an educational Renaissance. The educational effort was just as fundamental as the economic effort because it used the talents of the German people more effectively. The Allied Control Council's Directive #54 (1947), had insisted upon equality of elementary and secondary stages in schools; democratic organization of government and civil life; compulsory attendance to the age of fifteen followed by part-time attendance until eighteen; training of university status for teachers and free textbooks and tuition for all with maintenance grants for needy cases. The position of *Reichminister* of education had been abolished and the nine political divisions or *Länder* of West Germany given independent control of their educational futures with a *Kultusminister* in each *Land*. Each of the *Länder* set up a basic school code, so that there were nine different systems of education in West Germany. This diversity had value, but now the Germans are engaged in making sure that certain uniform agreements in education will permit children to transfer from one part of the country to another without disadvantage. Now the divisions total eleven.

The *Rahmenplan* (or Framework Plan) of the German Committee for Education was of paramount importance since it concentrated upon the transformation and the unification of the general public school system. In addition, the *Empfehlungen des Wissenschaftsrates* (or Recommendations of the Science Council) for the building up of higher education constituted basic outlines for the German renaissance in education. First the *Rahmenplan* helps to meet the need for adjusting the German educational system to the tremendous social and cultural upheavals of the past fifty years. After five years' preparation, the German Committee on Education submitted the plan in February, 1959. The experts of the Committee were very much aware of the tremendously increased "groundswell" (Dr. Edward Beeby's term) towards further schooling for everyone in secondary and higher education. Parents and children both desired to use education as a means of advancement to a higher social position. The new mobility in the German social structure could enable everyone to rise or fall through his own efforts in educational and in professional training. The experts wished to take into account the development of educational knowledge and of expansion of civilization in general. They also wished to reorganize education so that the *Grundschule* (elementary school) was retained as a base through the first four years, followed by the *Förderstufe* (advanced grades) through the sixth school year. This provided a continuous primary school and junior secondary school, and in reality extended the unified school up by the *Förderstufe* through the sixth school year. Upon this base they wished to rebuild the three traditional school types in a changed form. The old *Volkschule* was to become the *Hauptschule*, extending at once through the tenth year and eventually through the eleventh school year. The *Mittelschule* was to become the *Realschule*, extending from the end of the sixth through the tenth and then the eleventh year. The old *Höhere Schulen* now became two types of *Gymnasia,* one emphasizing science, the other modern language, beginning at the end of the sixth school year and extending through the thirteenth. To this was added the new nine-year *Studienschule* in two divisions, French and Greek, which began at the end of the fourth school year for specially gifted children. The German experts have recommended upward extension of the unified school so as to give all children a better chance. This delays the time of selection until later except for those who show unusual talent very early and are obviously capable of university studies. This plan resulted in much discussion and has the possibility of moving German education forward in a liberal way.

The Renaissance of the German education system was also advanced through the *Empfehlungen des Wissenschaftrats.* The experts conducting this study made certain recommendations for the improvement of German higher education. They pointed out that the ideal characteristics of German higher education had included close personal connection between the teacher and his student, the great systematic lectures surveying the problems in a research area, the seminars and laboratories for research, and freedom of teaching and learning. The Council examined other aspects of university education. The trend toward democratization of society in the present day has also led to the insistence that everyone should have the way open toward complete scientific education in accordance with his talents. Thus Germany faces increased pressures toward the expansion of higher education and of professional schools. A so-called second educational way (*Der Zweiten Weg*), provides access into scientific higher education outside the academic secondary schools. Some of the most fundamental recommendations included the conservation of the unity of research and teaching, sufficient professorships to maintain the universality and efficiency of education, the building up of certain areas and subjects at various universities, cooperative research team work, the creation of sufficient opportunities for all students to extend their education with no restrictions because of space or teaching facilities, and the building of student homes and dormitories in large numbers. The contemporary and older vintages of German higher education reacted in varied ways to these proposals, but they agreed on the need for action to regain the position of leadership held by Germany in higher education.

The Germans have always used their educational system as an instrument of national style. They are moving toward a more professional type of training for all types of work with opportunities provided for an aristocracy of talent. The Germans seem to be convinced that a new attitude toward world affairs and especially those of Europe is vital and must be directly founded upon an improved liberal system of education as well as a European economic union. And Germany holds a strategic position in the shaping of the future pattern of life in Europe.

Russia

Russia, or the Soviet Union, has been the scene of conflict between an historical drive for individual independence and a trend toward an ancient God-king ideology, which has manifested itself first in the adulation of the Tsar and later in the near-worship of Lenin and Marx. The Soviet educational strategy is to teach more and more of its children more broadly and more rigorously, under the Communist Party's centralized control. There is a firm belief in the Pavlovian theory of conditioning of the individual through environment and in what A. N. Whitehead called the "Gospels of Force and Uniformity."

The Soviet Union is the largest country in the world and includes within its continental boundaries one-sixth of the inhabited portion of the earth (8,649,798 square miles). It is more than twice as large as the countries ranking next in size—Canada, China, and the United States. The population numbered over 210 million at the beginning of the 1960's, or about thirty million more than that of the United States. Slavs of Indo-European origin made up approximately seventy-five per cent of the population, but there are 170 ethnic groups. Some 200 languages are spoken, with Russian as the official language.

Russia is a vast lowland stretching from the Baltic and Black Seas eastward to the Pacific Ocean with only one low range of mountains, the Urals, breaking this expanse. It is bordered by frozen tundra on the north and on the south and east by a broad belt of plateaus and mountains extending from the Caucasus to the mountains of Central Asia and China. A great deal of Russia's area is not arable and the climate encompasses great extremes of temperature in summer and winter. The Soviet Union constitutes the dominant Communist state of the world, with a level of technology and industrial production second only to that of the United States.

The great historians of Russia—from Schiemann, Kluchevsky, and Pares, to their contemporary colleagues—have delineated the major shifts in Russian development. The eastern Slavs were a freedom-loving people of the forest and the rivers. Not long after the time of Charlemagne, Rurik, the leader of a tribe of Varangarians or Northmen called *Rus,* came to rule the Slavs. In 900 A.D. Christianity was introduced by Greek Orthodox missionaries and the use of the Cyrillic alphabet was adopted for the Russian language. The city of Kiev became a center of civilization. Moscow was settled by 1147. The first European impact upon Russia was soon followed by the definitive Asiatic impact.

The Tatars or Mongols invaded Russia and conquered it by 1240, establishing permanent control by settlement on the lower Volga River. The Russians under Alexander Nevsky defeated the Teutonic Knights (the German monastic order of knights) and the Swedes in the west, but the Mongols maintained their control from the east for over two hundred years until Ivan III (the Great) ended the tribute to the Tatars in 1480. The Russians then began their great period of eastward expansion with Ivan IV (the Terrible) who conquered Tatar strongholds in Kazan and beyond at the end of the sixteenth century. The Romanov dynasty began in the seventeenth century and alternated cycles of attraction toward the European and the Asiatic ways of life. The Cossack, Yermak, spearheaded the conquest of Siberia and the Russians reached the Pacific in 1640.

Peter the Great (1689–1725) opened the Russian windows on Europe, founding St. Petersburg (later Leningrad) and introducing European culture and education by decree. A German princess became Catherine the Great. She Europeanized Russia still further introducing the foundations of the European elite education. In the early nineteenth century the Russians forced Napoleon to retreat from Moscow and joined Metternich's reactionary alliance. The nineteenth century also brought a golden age in Russian literature and art including such names as Pushkin, Dostoevsky, Tolstoi,

Gogol and Tschaikowsky. The Russians pioneered in industrial arts and technical education. The building of the Trans-Siberian Railroad was a great technological achievement (1891–1905). Russia was an expansive force ("the bear that walks like a man") in conflict with Great Britain, France, Turkey, and later Japan for warmwater ports. The Tsars of Russia were still absolute monarchs but were torn by the conflict between the liberal revolutionary influence of Europe and oriental despotism. Alexander II was a liberal ruler who emancipated the serfs in 1861 and supported the North in the time of our Civil War. In his reign Vladivostok was founded on the Pacific and Alaska was sold to the United States in 1867. His successors often used their military forces and secret police to suppress social, political, and educational progress.

These historical shifts underlined the fluctuations between the European ideal of personal independence and the ancient Asiatic trend toward absolute control by a God-king. At the beginning of the twentieth century the First Russian Revolution followed the loss of the Russo-Japanese War in 1905, and was repressed. In March, 1917, the Second Russian Revolution succeeded in setting up a constitutional democratic government under the leadership of Kerensky and the Moderates. In November, the radical Bolsheviks took over, under Lenin, and set up a Communist dictatorship. Under Lenin and Trotzky's leadership, the Bolsheviks won the Civil War and were successful against Allied intervention from 1918 to 1920. Lenin ruled from 1918 to 1924 as leader of the Communist Party and encouraged educational reform. In the first stage of Soviet education there was a relatively open situation with utilization of Western progressive methods. Lenin and his wife, N. Krupskaya, were vitally interested in American education and much attracted by the idea of the "work school" developed by Georg Kerschensteiner in Germany. "Polytechnization" was a popular concept linking life and work with education. At first there was no central control of education by a ministry and local ideas and self determination were encouraged. Stalin succeeded him and became one of the most absolute dictators that the world has ever seen. He used education and propaganda as weapons to build up a new state of "Iron Pioneers," eliminating the previous educational experimentation and turning toward a rigorous education based upon the older European and Tsarist two-track, elite-mass system. The Russians used education with science and technology as primary weapons to improve the level of their culture.

All of the long-range factors in the Soviet Union are closely inter-woven into the Communist theory of government. The state-owned economy is based upon a series of overarching plans, the *Gosplan*. A series of Five-Year Plans began in 1928; the third was inter-rupted by World War II. Khrushchev abandoned the Sixth Five-Year Plan, since production goals could not be met, and substituted a Seven-Year Plan to run from 1959 to 1965 with the purpose of passing and surpassing the United States. The Soviets have set up a new version of the pyramid of elite-mass control and it is reminiscent of Plato's *Republic* with Spartan and Roman characteristics. The fifteen Soviet Socialist Republics are ruled by a dual governmental structure, an official government, which is in turn controlled by the Communist Party. The Soviet constitution says that the Socialist State is a people's democracy and that the Communist Party is the leader of the people in a centrally planned economy.

The elite organization of the Communist Party constitutes only four per cent of the population and rules the government through the Central Committee headed by its First Secretary. A vast and well-paid higher bureaucracy has grown up since the Revolution, made up of the Communist Party upper strata, the high officials of the State, armed services officers, plant managers, scientists, pro-fessors, artists, and writers. This is the "New Class" described by Djilas of Jugoslavia as the new exploiters of the masses. Their special privileges include official automobiles, improved living space, *dachas* or vacation houses, and attendance at the best schools for their children. Officially the Soviets are committed in their edu-cational system to giving everybody equal opportunity, making sure that only a competent elite comes to the top. However, within their system, the children of Party members obtain a favored position educationally and socially. All citizens must live in strict adherence to the Communist Party line which formulates the Soviet national style. The Party line shifts with the alterations in Party theories and educational strategy shifts with it.

The basic educational philosophy of Marxism states that the future can be controlled by manipulating the economic environ-ment. The environment is all-powerful and can be improved by advances in the means of production. There is little cherished concern for the individual personality.

Stalin's strategy of education extended from 1928 to his death in 1953 and emphasized a formal subject-matter and elite-mass system of education. The Four-Year School, starting at age seven, was the foundation or elementary school. The Seven-Year and Ten-Year Schools were set up to coordinate secondary and higher education. (Soviet education was organized into the following stages: the preschool for three- to seven-year-olds; the elementary school for seven- to ten-year-olds (it was taught in the native language of the area), and the junior secondary school for the twelve- to fourteen-year-olds.) The first seven grades were placed in the same building wherever possible and called a Seven-Year School. Many rural areas possessed only the four-year elementary school. The fourth stage, or senior secondary school, included students through age seventeen. The Ten-Year Schools in larger population centers contained all ten grades. The Soviet Schools thus constituted a 4–3–3 system. A selective division into three streams was made at age fourteen, the actual end of compulsory education. The largest group with the least academic talent was drafted into the labor reserve for work in factories and collective farms with part-time continuation schools. The second, more talented group was entered in the semiprofessional schools or technicums for training "middle grade" technicians in industry, in agriculture, in crafts, in business, in medicine, and in teaching. The ablest intellectual group with the highest marks in examinations went on to the senior secondary stage, and could qualify for universities and higher institutes.

Khrushchev became Premier in 1958, the year after the first artificial earth satellite was orbited by the Russians. He began the elimination of the Stalinist personality cult and at the same time instituted certain reforms in education, though the general pattern was maintained. Khrushchev spearpointed a trend toward closer ties between life and school and the further extension of public education in the Soviet Union. He revived the "polytechnic" idea that education should include experience with different types of work and provide a career interest for the rest of life as well as formal academic training. Emphasis was reintroduced upon "learning by doing" as in Lenin's time rather than memorized scholastic learning alone. The reforms emphasized entrance into higher education not only through academic excellence but also by contribution to the common good through socialized work. Khrushchev also went further along the line of State control by instituting increased numbers of residential schools. Increased work in laboratory, handicrafts, and mechanical and agricultural training was designed to meet the problem of drop-outs from school because of boredom and lack of interest. In 1959–60 other steps were taken to provide eight years' compulsory education for all children in both general and polytechnical knowledge. The Ten-Year Schools were reorganized into general secondary polytechnical schools. The official philosophy was oriented toward making the students competent in both general and polytechnic subjects, building up a love of work and active participation in Socialist activities, and furthering a Socialist aesthetic, physical, and moral education.

The Soviet strategy of education has retained in the main the ruthless efficiency of the past in producing competent manpower for the Soviet State but has broadened educational opportunities for a wider range of careers. There seems to be a definite dichotomy between the Soviet schooling of the very young which follows the best principles of child care through the preschool and kindergarten and the Spartan education in elementary, secondary, and higher education. Teaching and learning have been given high prestige in the Soviet Union, for Soviet leaders are rightly convinced that excellence in education is basic to national success. The higher education system, including the great general universities of Moscow and Leningrad and the general universities in each of the fifteen republics, has continued to progress. In addition over 800 specialized institutes of higher education have been developed with standing and prestige equivalent to that of the *Grandes Écoles* of France. The universities and institutes of higher education have concentrated their efforts upon the production of scientists, technologists, and engineers who make up about sixty per cent of all higher education graduates (as against some fifty per cent in England and twenty-five per cent in the United States). The rise of higher education in the Soviet Union has accelerated and may overtake the West. Coeducation has been reinstituted in Russia and women hold top posts in all fields of endeavor. The Russians have paid their highest prestige awards not only to their top-level administrators, statesmen, and business managers, but also to their university teachers and teachers in general. The Soviet system has constituted a real advance for its millions of citizens, bringing about the elimination of illiteracy and the production of an elite group of scientists, technologists, and professionals, together with a very broad foundation of trained technicians.

From the point of view of affluent Western nations, Soviet life has been austere and drab under the ruthless whip of competition. Many developing Asiatic and African nations are dazzled by the fact that Soviets have demonstrated an educational strategy and national style able to compete with the United States and other top industrial countries and to pioneer in space exploration.

The educational systems of England, France, Germany, and the USSR have exerted a world influence in shaping variants of educational strategy capable of coping with paramount issues in human civilization. Some very significant educational systems have also been developed in smaller countries, such as Denmark and Switzerland. In the mid-nineteenth century extraordinary Bishop Grundtvig of Denmark was distressed by the relative somnolence of his country and was impressed by the vitality of England's growth in technology, economics, and government. He returned to Denmark and led a national educational Renaissance, concentrating upon the development of a system of further schooling for young adults, the Folk High School. Within these schools he built up a curriculum emphasizing the strength and glory of Denmark in the past taught through folk songs, literature, and art. He combined intellectual emphasis with the improvement of technical skills, especially in the realm of agriculture. The result of his labors was to create a new national style and to make Denmark one of the most delightful countries of the world with one of the highest standards of living despite the fact that its material resources were relatively limited.

Switzerland also supports the basic thesis of the need for diversity and the capacity of small countries to make great contributions to the advancement of learning and of human happiness. As one of the first democracies of the world, it has contributed markedly to education's role as a primary instrument in the strategy of advancing national welfare. Pestalozzi was the Swiss pioneer in the new era of education, presenting the teacher as a kindly and wise mentor rather than as a Spartan disciplinarian. Switzerland built up one of the finest educational systems and with it one of the highest standards of living in the world. Italy, Spain, and other European countries have also made significant contributions to education. Europe's very diversity constitutes a historical witness to the necessity of a wide range of free educational systems growing out of the historical evolution of the national culture.

CHAPTER III

Education in Asian Culture Areas

Asia is a mountain-hearted continent; its mountain ranges extend outward from the "Roof of the World," the Pamirs, to enclose many ancient culture areas—China, Tibet, India, and Iran. The mountain ridges extend further out into the Indian Ocean and the Pacific to form the island culture areas of Japan, the Philippines, and Indonesia.[1] Asia has been a cradle of civilizations with distinctive characteristics, and the ability to gain from acculturation and to radiate their own cultural richness outward. China, Japan, and India each offer special opportunities for the study of educational strategy and national style in Asia.

China

The *leit motif* of Chinese history has been the essential continuity of its education and culture despite dynastic cycles and long periods of civil conflict. The perennial pattern in China has been one of civil strife and chaos, rise of a dynasty under a strong ruler, flowering of a distinctive culture, gradual decline into another epoch of civil strife, and then the rise of another dynasty. Throughout their history, the Chinese have always had a hunger for land, a desire for the preservation of individual dignity and independence, a reverence for learning, and familial loyalty. Education has played a major role in Chinese continuity.

Today China has an area of almost 3,800,000 square miles and a population of over 670 million—or close to one-fourth the total population of the world. The areas of the United States and China are roughly similar in size, but the Chinese population is more than three times that of the United States. Lofty mountain ranges encircle its northern, western, and southern borders and have given China a protected cultural citadel. Continental China presents challenging climatic extremes. North China is a land with a cold climate and

---

[1] Dudley Stamp, *Asia* (London: Methuen, 1950), pp. 1ff.

raises hard grains. The camel caravans and the creaking wheels of carts have cut deep roads into the windblown soil strata of the plateau. In contrast, South China is a land with a warm monsoon climate characterized by the cultivation of rice and the extensive use of boats on the waterways and river systems. The chief religions of China include Confucianism, Taoism, and Buddhism. The largest province of China, Sinkiang, has a population which is eighty per cent Moslem. There are small minorities of Christians and Jews. The Chinese language has many dialects, the most important being Mandarin, whose standard form is Pekinese. In addition some of the other important dialects are Hakka, Cantonese, Foochow, and Swatow. The thirty thousand ideographic characters used at present in written Chinese, together with the many dialects, present a major educational problem.

The civilization of China began before 2000 B.C. At that time the Chinese people were already tilling land, taming animals, and making pottery. Certain dynasties provide perspective in the development of Chinese culture and education. Three famous teachers—Confucius, Lao Tse, and Mencius—lived during the Chou Dynasty (1027–479 B.C.). Confucius was the great teacher of the fifth century B.C. who set up an ethical ideal for the Chinese civilization. He taught men the virtues which should characterize "the superior man": benevolence, kindness, devotion, and tolerance. He emphasized education's role in molding the minds of men. Confucius said "Let us purify our hearts, correct our morals and go back to the old ways and loyalties." His teachings encouraged devotion to the ways of the ancestors and undergirded the family and clan loyalties of the Chinese people which have survived so many dynastic changes.

The period of civil war which followed the decline of the Chou Dynasty ended with the rise to power of Emperor Shi Wang Ti. Shi Wang Ti was a totalitarian ruler whose methods foreshadowed those of Mao Tse Tsung. He not only built the Great Wall against nomadic invaders from the north but also exercised a strict censorship, burning classic books which might produce "dangerous" thinking. He standardized forms of writing, codes of law, the axle length of carts, and the coinage. Populations were shifted where the government wished. Political offenders and drafted settlers were used to fill up new virgin lands in the outer edges of the Empire and especially in South China.

Shi Wang Ti's brief empire collapsed after fourteen years and was succeeded by the great Han Empire which lasted from 202 B.C. to 220 A.D. (approximately the same time span as the Roman Empire). The religious and ethical system of Confucianism was revived and established as an official creed. During the Han dynasty, Chinese control was expanded into Central Asia and Tibet. This dynasty warded off the invading Huns and created a great new civilization. It built up a class of scholarly administrators, the Mandarins, who lived according to the Confucian ethics. The Chinese extended-family and clan system continued and within this context there was an opportunity for the individual to rise. A Chinese elite educational system gradually evolved which trained competent high-level bureaucrats through a system of state examinations. This strategy of education was based upon provincial schools in which talented students of every social class were encouraged to study for a government career. Clans, families, and communities helped support worthy candidates for the state examinations. By the second century A.D., printing was developed and Buddhism was brought over the mountains from India and became another important factor in Chinese civilization.

Eventually the Han dynasty declined and a new dynasty—the Tang—arose. The Tang Empire expanded China's territory aggressively to its greatest extent including Siberia, Central Asia, Tibet, and Southeast Asia. China was probably the most powerful country in the world at that time. Its rulers improved the system of examinations for civil service and perfected the Mandarinate. This dynasty was pre-eminent in every field of art.

A succession of other dynasties were founded. Then the invading Mongols took over the control of China in the thirteenth century. Kublai Khan and other rulers of this foreign dynasty were able to rule China only with the assistance of the Mandarian bureaucracy. Marco Polo and other travelers reported the high level of Chinese civilization in the thirteenth century. The elite education system worked efficiently in producing competent scholars, artists, technologists, and administrators. The Mongol control was terminated by the Ming dynasty which lasted from the end of the fourteenth century until the middle of the seventeenth century. Then Manchu invaders from the north set up an empire which lasted from 1644 to 1911. The old elite system of education gradually broke down. There was not a sufficient foundation for the demands of the new democracy and technology of the nineteenth century. Dr. Sun Yat-Sen led a revolution in 1911 which resulted in the establishment of the Chinese Republic.

The Republic of China began to build up a modern school system on the 6–3–3 plan with a basic six-year elementary education, a three-year junior high school, and a three-year high school. Education was compulsory from ages six to twelve. There was provisional establishment of a comprehensive type of academic high schools but after five years it was abolished by the Ministry of Education and the separate secondary schools were reinstituted: academic, vocational, and normal. The universities gradually attained international prestige. The Christian missionary contribution to the evolution of modern education in the Republic of China was distinguished both in the movement for general literacy and in the formation of schools and universities. John Dewey and many foreign consultants were impressed by Chinese advances in modern education and culture. At the same time the Chinese Renaissance in modern literature was in process, especially in the universities. Hu Shih led this movement toward a simplification of the difficult Chinese language and the writing of literature in the popular idiom so that it could be understood by a greater number of people. Jimmy Yen, coming out of a YMCA background, was a significant leader in the fight against illiteracy, a fight which made noteworthy progress.

The Japanese invasion of the 1930's was stoutly resisted by the Chinese. They moved their major governmental controls and educational centers westward. The battle for survival of higher education in China 1937–45 was an extraordinary undertaking. The professors and their students moved westward under great difficulties to the southwestern province of Yunnan. Higher education was carried out in a very primitive environment. The Japanese invasion was eventually repulsed, but the collapse of the Republic of China before Communist pressures soon followed. Many students and professors fled from China or remained abroad (one of them was C. N. Yang, the nuclear physicist and Nobel Prize winner).

In 1949–50 the Communist People's Republic of China took

over the mainland, bringing with it a shift in national style and educational strategy. The Party Line, expounded by Mao Tse Tsung, became the official policy. The character of education was to be "national, scientific, and popular," raising the level of all, especially peasants and workers to "become constructive citizens of the new Socialist State." In February, 1956, a thirty-letter version of the Roman alphabet was adopted. The Communist Five-Year Plans of 1953–57 and 1958–62 set up targets for educational achievement, including elimination of illiteracy, establishment of universal elementary education, and acceleration of secondary and higher education with emphasis upon a close linkage between productive work and learning. The 6–3–3–4 educational system remained nominally as developed before 1949, but stress was placed on shortening the twelve-year school to a ten-year unitary school of general education which would not compete with manpower needs. University courses were also shortened. Entrance to secondary schools and universities was by competitive examinations. The People's Republic drove toward expansion of an efficient elite-mass type of education resembling that of the Soviet Union. *The Great Ten Years,* published by the Peking government in 1960, described their official view of a decade of progress. Education is viewed as a primary and indispensable weapon for advancement of the Socialist State.

Japan

The Japanese strategy of education and national style has been a pattern of independent and intelligent acculturation. Largely as a result of its educational progress, Japan has become the most highly westernized of Asia's major lands. Japan has played a paramount role in the conflict between democracy and dictatorship which is so interwoven in the fates of both East and West.

Japan has a population of over 90 million people in an area of only approximately 143,000 square miles. Japan is a huge complex of four large islands. If one superimposed Japan on the eastern United States, the southernmost island, Kyushu, would be in the same latitude as Georgia, the heart of Japan around Tokyo would parallel North Carolina, and the northernmost island, Hokkaido, would be in the same latitude as New Hampshire. The two central islands are Honshu and Shikoku, enclosing the Inland Sea. The favorable mild maritime climate of Japan permits the raising of a wide variety of crops. Japan, however, is a very mountainous country with a rugged coast line, leaving the Japanese farmer only about twenty per cent of the total land as arable. The Japanese have become one of the greatest seafaring people of Asia, with their own Inland Sea giving them their take-off point for the oversea routes.

In early days, water barriers were even greater because of the difficulties of navigation and Japan had an isolation from which it could choose to emerge or into which it could choose to retire. Japan was able to borrow what it wished and to create a new pattern and form of civilization which was distinctive and indigenous.[2] The Japanese are not imitators but ingenious innovators who engaged in an intelligent process of acculturation. This theme of cultural isolation and contact is very important in analyzing Japan's national style and strategy of education.

The first wave of Mongoloid invaders from Korea probably reached Japan in the first century A.D. The invaders came in waves pushing up the highway of the Inland Sea to the central part of Honshu. Here in the small Yamato plain one clan grew strong and this Yamato clan's priest-chief gradually gained supremacy over other clan chiefs. From the Yamato priest-chief grew the God-kings of the Japanese imperial family. Japanese civilization has been basically under one ruling family's control for the past fifteen hundred years.

The first great period of Japanese education and culture developed in the seventh century A.D. as the result of contact with the Tang Empire. Japan was a child of the Chinese civilization but the Japanese transformed and adapted the Chinese civilization to their own pattern of life. As early as 552 B.C., the Buddhist religion was brought from a kingdom of southern Korea to the Yamato clan as a vehicle for educational contact. Buddhism was an aggressive missionary religion making many converts and also extending Chinese culture. Crown Prince Shotuku led the victory of the Buddhist religious group in Japan and sent a large official embassy to China in 607. As they did later on in the Meiji period, the Japanese chose their best people to go on the series of embassies: artists, scholars, skilled and sensitive young men who already had knowledge of

---

2 Edwin O. Reischauer, *Japan, Past and Present* (New York: Alfred A. Knopf, Inc., 1946), pp. 10ff.

China. They went with the embassies and often remained for a decade in China to study and then brought back to the isolated islands of Japan the glory of the Tang Empire's civilization in ethics, politics, technology, science, art, and literature.

Unfortunately, the Chinese writing system accompanied these valuable acquisitions. The Chinese writing system had a special symbol, an ideograph to represent each word-root or word of one syllable. The Japanese used classical Chinese almost as the Europeans of the Middle Ages used Latin—for everything from law books and documents to histories. The Japanese gradually developed a syllabary or *kana* using Chinese characters as phonetic symbols. This was not as efficient as an alphabet but nevertheless it gave the Japanese a way of writing their own language. The Japanese today are struggling with the problem set up at that time, the combination of a phonetic syllabary with a heavy introduction of Chinese characters for uninflected individual words. As a result, the Japanese writing system became a roadblock for both the technical and intellectual growth of modern Japan.

While the court families at Kyoto were creating literature and art in the tenth and eleventh centuries, the provincial aristocrats were setting up a new feudal society. These knights on horseback were ruling their peasants and learning how to manage their estates. They resembled the medical knights of Europe and, like them, acquired a military education which affected the evolution of modern Japanese education and culture. Thus began almost seven centuries of political control by a military feudal class.

A great religious educational renaissance accompanied the political transformation. The scribes, or Buddhist priests, assumed increased importance to match that of the warriors. Buddhism was transformed by the Chinese and the Japanese from a search for Nirvana, in which the ego of the individual was absorbed into the cosmos with all desire overcome, into an optimistic attitude concerning the peace and beauty of life. They regarded human life as essentially good and not as something to escape from. Buddhism assumed a new form and simultaneously became adventurous in commerce. The profits of these trading exploits paid not only for beautiful temples but also for the bronze Great Buddha at Kamakura set up toward the end of the thirteenth century. Japanese medieval guilds manufactured a rich variety of goods and with it an overseas trade grew up. Japanese traders were dominant as far as Manila and Siam. From the twelfth to the sixteenth century the Japanese built themselves up from a small, economically weak land at the outer fringes of the civilized world into an advanced far-voyaging nation.

Japan now went into another cycle of isolation in 1600 (at the very time that England—another island power—was entering a period of expansion). In that year, Tokugawa Ieyasu operating out of his castle headquarters in Edo, a village on the site of the future metropolis of Tokyo, defeated his rival. He and his successors began the period of Tokugawa political stability based upon rigid control of society, suppression of the creative trends, and a return to reactionary forms of feudalism. The Tokugawa encouraged the study of early Chinese Confucianism as a stabilizing philosophy of government. The hierarchy was made up of four social classes: the warrior, the peasant, the artisan, and the merchant. The top class of warriors, called *Samurai,* were also administrators. The merchants were placed last despite their great importance because, according to Confucian theory, they were unproductive. The Tokugawa suppressed their own adventurous overseas traders as well as Christian missionaries. This period of withdrawal and consolidation came to an end in the nineteenth century because of a cultural transformation from within, including the rise of the merchant class and cities, and because of the penetration from the Western world.

Modern Japan began in 1868 with the Meiji Period and renewed cultural contact with the world. The American government had opened the gates of Japan to trade with a naval squadron under Commander Perry. The young Samurai of western Japan had conquered and taken over the stable Tokugawa government almost intact by 1867. They began a revolutionary modernization planned and carried out from on top. In January, 1868, this oligarchic government restored the young emperor to official power and direct rule, giving the period the name Meiji. This era came to be known as the Meiji Restoration. The young leaders moved the capital from Kyoto to Edo, which was renamed Tokyo or "the eastern capital." These leaders were military men but they understood that if Japan wished to be militarily strong it must have a complete intellectual, social, political, and economic transformation. The Meiji rulers carried out one of the greatest transformations in one of the briefest periods the world has ever seen.

They turned the world into one vast school and learned what they chose from it, using the criteria of excellence and efficiency. The United States was studied for business methods and education, France for law and education, Germany for the army, medicine, and education, and England for the merchant marine and navy. They recognized the need for modern state reorganization including religious tolerance, modern currency, police, and postal and civil service. The development of a well-chosen educational strategy was of paramount importance to them because they understood that education is a primary instrument in the advance of the modern state and its national style. Therefore the oligarchy organized a Ministry of Education in 1871 and began an advanced program of educational expansion. They set up a two-track system with universal elementary education and a six year compulsory school for all. Above this were the middle schools and higher schools leading to the universities which produced higher government officials, scientists, scholars and doctors. There were set up eight collegiate divisions in Japan, each of which had a university. Education was regarded by government as an instrument to train obedient servants of the state. At first the Japanese were impressed by the American school system and followed its trend toward making a practical education available to everyone, but by 1880 the European and Confucianist conservative pattern gained power.

Within fifty years after the "Restoration" Japan had become one of the five great industrial and military powers of the world. Illiteracy was practically abolished. An efficient government backed up a strong industry, military forces, and a disciplined and technically trained citizenry. At the same time Japan had moved in the direction of liberal democracy, though this was not apparent on the surface. The Christian missionaries brought the ideals of the West and won converts among the intellectual classes who exerted notable influence on Japanese life. During World War I, businessmen became powerful figures, tending to compete with the military. They preferred progress through trade and wanted to cut the high cost of the military establishment. The city dwellers were expanding and the new generation of highly educated teachers, doctors, lawyers, writers, office workers, and university professors were in touch with the liberal trends of the Western world. In 1925 the entire adult male population of Japan received the vote and at the same time union membership grew. The great earthquake and fire in the Tokyo area on September 1, 1923, cleared the way for a new urban culture. Despite the persistence of male-dominated family solidarity, women began to rise to social equality. The Japanese became sports enthusiasts. Baseball was already the national sport and it was joined by track and field sports, swimming, golf, tennis, and skiing. The Japanese cultural Renaissance advanced with the publication of thousands of books and extensive translation of the literature of the entire world. The new urban classes moved in the direction of the rich democratic cultural life of the Western world and were in conflict with the controlled transformation of Japan into a strong industrial and military power by the oligarchs.

In the 1930's a powerful militaristic and nationalistic reaction took place under the leadership of army and navy officers linked with the peasantry, rural landowners, small town dwellers, and minor government officials. These men had been heavily affected by the earlier totalitarian indoctrination of the school system. Many of the new officer caste came from peasant rural landowners and officer backgrounds and they led a direct attack upon the new democratic trends. They controlled thought, forcing university and higher school students into memorization patterns similar to those of the lower schools, depriving the women of their new emancipation, and suppressing newspapers' freedom of expression. Militarists made a coalition with the great business groups, the *Zaibatsu,* and were able to take control away from the party politicians and moderates. This militaristic leadership of Japan moved rapidly into the Manchurian Incident, the attack upon China, and World War II.

Japan began one of the most extraordinary phases of its long history with its military surrender on September 2nd, 1945. There began the American occupation which was to last for six and a half years of control and guidance. Both the Americans and Japanese can take credit for the unusual experiment in acculturation which took place. The United States had both a wise policy and a wise administrator: General Douglas MacArthur. The aggressive reforms of the American occupation had a success which can be explained only by the firm democratic trends already underway in Japan, the presence of universal education, and the Japanese desire for a change from reactionary leadership which had ruined Japan. The occupation engaged in educational reforms, not all of which will endure. The decentralization of control in the school system is currently in the process of reversal. The establishment of a single-track system of education was carried out with a six-year elementary school, a three-year lower secondary school, and a three-year upper secondary school leading to the university and higher education. The Japanese have already begun to return to their more selective secondary and higher education pattern. The requirement of compulsory education for nine years (covering the elementary and lower secondary schools) persists. Extensive changes in curriculum and methodology led to controversy. The more systematic teaching of subject matter was reinstituted. Increased emphasis has reappeared upon instruction in morals and manners, expansion of scientific and technical education, improved vocational training, and the fundamental processes of reading, writing, and computing. The democratization and liberalization of educational opportunity, however, have left a permanent impress.

The long-range factors in Japanese educational strategy and national style are more clearly seen through the perspective of history. It would seem that Japan has emerged from a reactionary period and will continue to pursue democratic liberal trends but will still face certain nostalgia for the traditional past. The Japanese not only learned Western technology, science, and business methods, but also experienced the conflict between totalitarian autocracy and democratic liberal life. Much of the future of Asia and of the world will depend upon what happens within the extraordinary civilization of Japan.

India

The huge triangular subcontinent of India has witnessed many epochs of intrusion, synthesis and outward expansion of culture. India has absorbed a succession of conquerors by land and sea and has evolved its own unique civilization. India is about one-seventh the size of the Soviet Union, but her population is almost twice that of the latter. India constitutes one of the major strategic keys to Asia's future and the world. Although the center of Hindu culture for thousands of years, the new nation of India began in 1947, when it gained independent status as a self-governing federal republic in the British Commonwealth. The survival and progress of India as a great democracy is vital to the entire world. India is engaged in creating a new national style and strategy of education in order to attack the primary problems of mankind, present here in "critical mass," expanding population, land-use reform, religion and superstition, social structure and conflict, health and disease. India's possible success in creating a new synthesis of ancient liberal education and modern vocational specialization in her educational system is vital to us all.

India's growth and development as a civilization have been influenced by such long-range factors as her land, which is divided into three great regions: the Himalayan area, the northern river plains, and the southern tableland. The mountain region of the north extends from the Hindu-Kush through the Himalayas over into the mountain ranges of Southeast Asia. The mountains have been penetrated by invaders chiefly through the Northwest Frontier's Khyber and Bolan passes. Through these passes the Indo-Europeans migrated to drive back the original Dravidian inhabitants beyond the Satpura and the Vindhaya Mountain Ranges which border the region of the Deccan Plateau of the south. Thereafter the Satpura line has marked a cultural division between the languages and racial types of the Indo-European north and the Dravidian south. Between these two regions lies the Indo-Gangetic Plain, stretching from the lowlands of the Ganges Delta to Delhi and then through the Indus Valley and the Thar Desert to the Arabian Sea. The climate of India is in general a monsoon type with alternating rainy and dry seasons, but temperature varies greatly from the cold mountain ranges of the north to the subtropical and tropical lands of the center and the south. India is ninety per cent agricultural, a land of villages living close by the wild life of the jungle, plains, and forests.

The historical development of India's education and culture divides itself into certain major phases. The early Pre-Dravidian civilizations, including the culture of Mohenjo Daro along the Indus, were as old as those of the other great river valley civilizations of China, Mesopotamia, and Egypt. A tremendous migration of the Indo-Europeans pressed forward from the north into India around 2000 B.C. to the Satpura Mountain Line and were transformed into a caste-structured society. They created some of the world's finest literature, the Vedas, and also the religion of Hinduism with its pantheon of gods and search for Nirvana. Buddhism began a splendid epoch in Indian cultural history in the fifth century B.C., and was marked by a vigorous missionary expansion. Buddha's teaching of the Middle Way with its ethical, aesthetic, and educational implications was carried by missionaries into Tibet, China, Japan, and Southeast Asia. The priestly schools of Buddhism also evolved a memorable artistic heritage in the magnificent sculptures, shrines, temples, and paintings. The Buddhist ruler Asoka, who forswore war and pursued peace, was one of the most enlightened monarchs of all time. Asoka's wheel of life symbol is now part of the Indian national flag. Another intrusion from the northwest by the Greeks under Alexander the Great left a lasting impress upon art, language, and legend.

One of the most significant penetrations of India was that of Islam in the eighth century A.D. The Muslim invaders brought with them Persian culture and language and a great architecture (the influence of which is shown in the Taj Mahal). The invasion by Islam introduced a new monotheistic religion in conflict with the polytheism of the Hindus. The Muslim schools or *madrissahs* were open to a broad spectrum of the population. One of the major gifts of India to the world occurred during this period with the creation and transmission of the Indian numerals, including the zero or *sunya,* which became known as the Arabic numerals and gave us the beginnings of positional mathematics.

The next great intrusion by the Portuguese, English, and French came by sea and brought an advanced European technology to India. The English won control of the subcontinent in the eighteenth century, after they had lost their American colonies. Early in the nineteenth century they made the decision to use English rather than the vernacular in education, and thus opened up the technology, science, and art of the Western World to India. This step also made education a bookish literary preparation for civil servants. Increasingly the rising political, intellectual group of India became intent upon controlling its own future. The leadership of Gandhi and Nehru, the influence of the British parliamentary system, and the impact of the twentieth century in two world wars finally helped to bring about Indian independence in 1947.

The subcontinent was divided into the Republic of India and the Dominion of Pakistan, an Islamic federal republic made up of two geographical units separated by 1100 miles. The partition was a social cataclysm for Hindus and Muslims. The postpartition development of India as the first nonwhite dominion of the British Commonwealth has continued despite difficult and challenging problems.

India's educational and cultural advance is under accelerated impact by long-range factors. India is a theater for the conflict between the competing drives of the older literary, generalized, and agricultural world and the newer technological, industrial, specialized and urban world. The educational tradition has been largely literary, religious, and artistic, yet India needs above all concentration upon the educational tools provided by the natural sciences, the social sciences, and the professional areas of education, engineering, and medicine—particularly since the population of India has risen from about 50 million in 1800 to 400 million in 1960.

The imbalance of people and resources has been accentuated by certain customs and inheritances from the past such as the veneration of the cow, preventing its use as a source of food, and the sacredness of monkeys, which are free to destroy crops and food. The paramount problem of limiting the birth rate to balance the new decrease in the death rate is handicapped by custom, poverty, and lack of education. India has one of the lowest living standards in the world and is now eager that it be improved. In spite of her extensive problems, India has made progress through the series of Five-Year Plans which have given the government a chance to contribute markedly to economic, technological, social, and educational advance. The growth of private industrial enterprise has also aided markedly in India's development.

The Indians have one of the most ancient democratic organizations in the village council, or *panchayat*. The education of the *panchayat* to accept more responsibility for their village's future is essential to the progress of India which is still primarily a land of agricultural villages despite its growing urbanization. The extended-family system, with many relatives living in a large compound, has been a basic force in the lives of Indians. The caste system provided the basis of the social structure: from the Brahmin who had both a religious and educational function; the warrior, the merchant to the servant caste. Caste was economic as well as social providing for security in various jobs and careers. Those people without caste known as "untouchables" did the most menial tasks, but untouchability is now illegal.

Language is another problem in education, since India has at least twelve major regional languages with ancient literatures and two hundred minor languages. In 1949 it was decided to make Hindi the official national language. English was to be used for official purposes for fifteen years and was the language of communication in science and technology. The Sanskrit languages of the north (such as Hindi) are very different from the Dravidian languages (such as Telugu) south of the Satpura line. An educated Indian will need at least three languages; Hindi, English, and his regional language. Linguistic problems are stubborn, difficult, and basic to the solution of all other long-range factors in the culture.

India's present educational system is a combination of state and central government control. Each of the fourteen major states of India controls all education within its borders except technical and university education, which is controlled by the Central Ministry of Education. The constitution of India directs that all children up to the age of fourteen years must have free education, regardless of language, caste, religion, or race. The Indians have made the basic decision that education should be secular. This action should avoid religious strife and assist social reform. The Republic of India has a religious pattern approximately as follows: five per cent are Buddhists, Parsees, Jains, Jews, Sikhs and Christians; ten per cent are Muslims, and eighty-five per cent are Hindus.

In the course of operations the central government has had to take increasing responsibility for all aspects of education in order to provide uniform national goals and standards of operation. The fourteen states rely on the central government for financial subsidies, research and exchange of information. The central government's Five-Year Plans have included nationally integrated programs for education to meet All-India requirements. The detailed structure of education varies greatly from state to state but includes elementary education in the six to ten age group; secondary education in two stages, junior (or middle school, or lower secondary) for the ten to thirteen age group and senior (high school, higher secondary or multi-purpose schools) for the fourteen to seventeen age group. The successful secondary school graduates must pass through a two-year preuniversity preparation course at an intermediate college to gain entrance to the universities or can enter a polytechnic or vocational trade and industrial school directly. The universities have tended to dominate secondary education, making it college preparatory in character. A counterinfluence has come from Gandhi's "basic national education" of "heart and hand" which proposed the linkage of education with daily life and the learning of a craft. There is a conflict between the new realistic learning for living with emphasis on individual aptitudes and specialized training, and the traditional general literary learning which has been the pathway to higher status positions.

The Central Advisory Board, with the State Education Ministers and outstanding experts as members, exerts great power in planning a national educational strategy for coping with the long-range problems surveyed. The All-India Council for Technical Education has advanced technological and scientific training on a wide front in order to bring about an economy of abundance for India. The Indians have a strategic position in world education despite their vast problems. They have the capability of combining Western scientific technology and economic abundance with Indian philosophic tolerance and aesthetic sensitivity in an atmosphere of democracy. As Humayun Kabir said: "Communication and understanding are thus the essence of education, and a democracy offers the best medium where it can flourish."[3]

Other culture areas in Asia have made their own valuable indigenous contributions to the progress of education from the Republic of the Philippines and countries of Southeast Asia to Iran, Pakistan, and the Middle East.

The Republic of the Philippines has used Spanish and English as vehicles for the synthesis of their island cultures and that of Europe and America and has expanded a system of national education as a primary factor in its democratic national style.

At the other end of Asia the Republic of Turkey constitutes a bridge to Europe, geographically and culturally. In the 1920's, under the leadership of Mustafa Kemal, or Atatürk, the Turkish people carried out a dynamic revolution, modernizing their nation in

---

[3] H. Kabir, *Education in New India* (New York: Harper & Row, Publishers, 1955), p. 208.

little more than a generation. Atatürk's saying: "Knowledge is the truest guide in life" became a motto of educational reform. The Turkish state had an ideology which was republican, nationalist, populist, secular, and reformist, with state responsibility in economics and welfare. The reformist emphasis was shown in the adoption of the Roman alphabet in 1928 to break a link with the past and to combat illiteracy more effectively by facilitating the teaching of reading and writing.

CHAPTER IV

Education in African Culture Areas

The continent of Africa has possessed great significance in the past and will possess even more in the future. It is a land of diversity, from the primitive tribes of the central area to the ancient civilization of Egypt. The Mediterranean and Red Sea coasts have felt the impact of a succession of ancient civilizations: Egyptian, Cretan, Hittite, Assyrian, Persian, Greek, Phoenician, Roman and Teuton. The wave of Islam flowed across the northern third of Africa in the seventh century A.D., making the tribes part of a great Islamic civilization.

Sub-Sahara Africa remained separated into small tribal groups except for periodic conquests by dominant tribes such as the Ashanti, Fulani, and Zulu. In the fifteenth century, the Portuguese began a succession of European penetrations, followed by the Dutch and English, and, in the nineteenth century, the French and Germans. Today Africa is a continent of new nations emerging from ancient tribal patterns with an overlay of European languages and culture. All face the critical problem of producing high-level educated manpower with an adequate base of general literacy in order to cope with the accelerated growth of all the long-range factors essential to national development. Two culture areas offer particularly rich rewards in comparative study: Egypt and Nigeria. The first an ancient civilization; the second a young undeveloped country.

Egypt, the United Arab Republic

Egypt forms a bridge between Africa and Asia and holds a strategic position in the world of Islam and the Arab lands of the Near East. The Arab East has been desired by many races because of its control of trade routes, its favorable climate, and its wealth.

The Arab lands of the Near East have built their cultures upon successive waves of races, each invading and leaving a stratum of civilization. Present practices combine past strata. The Arabic language, and the religion and culture of Islam have been the heritage of these lands for over thirteen centuries and underneath is a firm base in the preceding cultures of the Near East. The early Egyptian and Mesopotamian river valley civilizations created the beginnings of Western or European civilization through innovations in agriculture, architecture, transportation, geometry, astronomy, a phonetic alphabet, and three primary monotheistic religions: Judaism, Christianity, and Islam. The trading voyages of the Semitic Phoenicians spread these cultural developments along the Mediterranean shores.

The Greeks learned from the Egyptian and Near Eastern cultures and created a golden age of their own. The Greek genius for innovation presented the world with original contributions in drama, architecture, art, literature, games, mathematics and philosophy. Then the Greeks advanced the frontiers of Hellenic civilization into Egypt, the Near East, and Central Asia. The Near East and Egypt were under the influence of Greek culture, reinforced by Rome and Christianity, for a thousand years. The rise of Islam in the seventh century A.D. welded together the Greco-Roman inheritance, submerged for centuries in Medieval Europe, with culture from Persia, India, and Egypt and returned it to Spain and southern Europe before the Crusades.

The Near East was laid desolate in the thirteenth century by the Mongol invasion, which was repulsed only by Egypt. A long period of decline followed. With the nineteenth century a Renaissance began in the Near East and the Arab world, stimulated by the returning currents of Western civilization. This Renaissance was accelerated in the twentieth century. Egypt has been a key figure in the modern development of Islam and the Arab World.

The ancient land of Egypt is dominated by the Nile River. Any traveler is impressed by the contrast between the living green of the Nile Valley and the surrounding desert. The land of Egypt includes some 386,000 square miles but the main inhabited area is limited to the Nile Valley with about 13,580 square miles. The population was over 26 million in the middle of the twentieth century and consists of three major elements. The Hamito-Semite race is the largest and is called the *Fellahin* (derived from *fellâh,* tiller of the soil), living in rural districts. The second major element includes the Arabs, or the *Bedawi.* Only a sixth of them are nomads; the others are partially sedentary in the Fayum Basin and in the cultivated outskirts of the delta and Nile Valley. The third, or Nubian, element lives between Aswan and Wadi Halfa in the upper Nile Valley and is of mixed Negro and Arab blood. Egypt's primary problem has always been population density. In the heavily populated Nile Valley the population density is approximately 2500 per square mile. The burden of the country has rested on the shoulders of the toiling farmer or *Fellahin*. The *Fellahin* is afflicted by many diseases including tracoma, bilhariasis, caused by the liver fluke and carried by the snails living in slow water, and virulent forms of malaria and other fevers.

The people of Egypt have shown ability and genius throughout their long history. From the times of Zozer's Pyramid at Sakkarah and the Great Pyramids of Gizeh, the scribes of Egypt demonstrated their skill in many realms of knowledge—medicine, mathematics, architecture, and literature. Egyptian accomplishments have included the invention of an alphabet, accurate computation of star tables, and mensuration of the river, its soil, its floods. The limitation of learning to a small elite priesthood was symbolized by the term *hieroglyphics* or sacred writings. The pharoah Ikhnaton contributed a noble and ethical monotheism at the time of the Hittites. One of the first great centers of learning in the world was the Hellenic university of Alexandria with its magnificent library and its competent researchers in the natural sciences and in the humanities which affected the subsequent intellectual history of the Mediterranean and Near Eastern area. The Roman occupation of Egypt was concerned with the advancement of education for the ruling elite in the towns and cities. As Rostovtzev pointed out, the Roman Empire's urban culture was too thin a veneer and through it, as in Egypt, the great rural culture and language blocks forced their way.

When Islam swept across the Near Eastern and Mediterranean world, the Koran became the primary source for all intellectual and cultural life. The *kuttab* was the immemorial ungraded Muslim school in which the children learned how to read, write, and figure. The Koran was recited aloud in unison, and memorized as the foundation of living and learning. Cairo, the capital of Egypt, became one of the great centers of Islamic culture. Its ancient university of al-Azhar was founded by the Fatimids in 970 A.D. The eleventh and twelfth centuries witnessed a further flowering of Islamic culture throughout the Near East but the Mongol invasion in the thirteenth century ruined many Muslim centers of population and learning. The Seljuk Turks were succeeded by the Ottomans, magnificent in war but tending to be reactionary in culture and education.

Toward the beginning of the nineteenth century, the national spirit of Egypt revived under the impact of increased European influence. The first viceroy of Egypt, Muhammad Ali Pasha, founder of the ruling dynasty of Egypt, created the basic structure of Egyptian education. He wished to build up a modern State with strong armed forces as rapidly as possible. In the 1830's the primary school system was created in order to supply the needed personnel for the rapidly expanding army and navy and the civil bureaucracy. In 1836–37 Muhammad Ali founded the central Ministry of Education, which controlled almost all education in Egypt. Its functions have been continued and enlarged ever since, except for a brief interruption during the regime of Sa'id Pasha. French influence was strong and the French language had a pre-eminent position in the curriculum. During his long rule he sent over three hundred students abroad, chiefly to France. Their major subjects for study in Europe were military and naval science, medicine, pharmacy, engineering, and such crafts as carpentry and printing. The university students sent abroad were later used by Muhammad Ali to replace European teachers and officials in schools, government departments, and the army. They translated technical books into Arabic and Turkish and served as national leaders, contributing to Egyptian progress. Muhammad Ali's armies became powerful enough to threaten the Ottoman Empire in Istanbul and he considered the idea of establishing an Arab Empire. A concert of European powers forced him to withdraw his armies from Syria and Asia Minor and to be content with ruling Egypt as Viceroy or Khedive. Egypt continued its semi-independent existence under the nominal but distant authority of the Sultan in Istanbul. The British conquest in 1887 stimulated the growth of Egyptian nationalism and led finally to the withdrawal of the British, the abdication of the ruling dynasty, and the rise of the revolutionary government of Gamel Abdel Nasser after World War II. Egyptian education developed its own significant form throughout the periods of political change.

The educational system of Egypt was a two-track organization for the elite and the masses. Free elementary schools were provided for the great majority of Egyptian children, but these did not prepare students for secondary and higher education. Only a few talented students were allowed to transfer to primary schools, originally set up by Muhammad Ali Pasha to train an elite rapidly and efficiently. The primary school began with kindergarten and continued through institutions of higher education. The primary schools were tuition schools until 1943.

The Egyptians, in contrast to other Arab lands, adapted the indigenous *kuttab* to modern needs, making it the basis of the elementary ladder. In 1869, the Ministry inspected the *kuttabs,* improved their curricula and transformed them gradually into the four-year standard elementary school (*maktab*). Two other types of elementary schools were added, one of five years and another of six. All types included instruction in reading, writing, basic arithmetic, and religion. Transfer to advanced standing in a primary school was possible for able students from the upper years of elementary school. The primary ladder had preparatory kindergartens with three grades, primary schools with four grades, secondary schools with five grades, and higher institutions—including universities—of four to six years. The primary schools accordingly began with eight year olds who could read, write and do arithmetic and who were prepared in kindergartens or transferred from elementary schools. The successful passing of public examinations was required for entrance into secondary and higher education. Three major modern universities were founded at Cairo, Alexandria, and Asyut in the twentieth century in addition to the ancient university of Al Azhar, the unrivalled center of Islamic learning.

In 1943, Minister of Education Al-Hilali Pasha not only abolished all primary school fees but ordered all secondary schools to admit students to vacant places on the basis of their levels of achievement in examinations without regard to fees. The results were twofold: private schools were gradually integrated into the public school system, and parents pressed for entrance of their children into the government primary and secondary schools which offered better instruction and educational and career opportunities. In the postwar years, Egypt moved further toward a unified school system: a compulsory six-year school for six- to twelve-year-olds, followed by a secondary school divided into two stages of three years each. The change took place first to a 4-4-3 and then to a 6-3-3 year system. Egypt, now the United Arab Republic, has traversed a long road of acculturation, preserving its own Islamic foundation and adapting modern developments in education to its own requirements. Emphasis has been placed upon combatting illiteracy and extending elementary education to the border areas as well as in the Nile valley proper. In secondary education the policy has been to expand technical and agricultural education. School libraries have been enriched and teacher training has been improved. The University of Cairo has enlarged its faculties and facilities. Technical education has been emphasized at the Universities of Alexandria and Asyut. The Egyptian revolution in education is perhaps exemplified by the recent unification within the ancient Al-Azhar University of the traditional Islamic studies with such modern faculties as law, medicine, education, and public administration—an experiment which will be viewed with great interest by the educational world. Egypt has been and will be a strategic force not only in the African continent and culture area but also in the southwest Asian culture area or Near East.

Nigeria

Nigeria has great cultural potentialities and constitutes a powerful factor in the future of Africa. This country is a rectangle of over 340,000 square miles and stretches along nearly 600 miles of the windswept Gulf of Guinea. The land rises from a sixty-mile coastal belt of mangrove swamp forest into a tropical rain forest zone of a hundred miles up to an arid and dry plateau 2000 feet above sea level. The plateau changes from woodland to tall grass savanna and reaches the southern edges of the Sahara. The people of Nigeria numbered close to 40 million in the early 1960's, with one of the highest population densities in Africa. A central factor in Nigeria's culture and education is the three regions which have been cut into its surface by the mighty Y of the Niger River flowing from the Sahara in the west and joined by the Benue flowing from the Cameroon Mountains in the east to make one huge stream which runs south to its delta in the Gulf of Guinea. The Western Region under the Niger has a population of approximately eight million, with the Yoruba tribe in the majority and among the most advanced Nigerians. They have a centuries-old tradition of political organization and two-thirds are Moslem or Christian. The Eastern Region under the Benue River has a population of about nine million with the Ibo tribe as its major group, half pagan, half Christian, and fiercely independent. These regions tend to control Nigeria's commerce and furnish many of the government officials. The most powerful region is the Northern Region above the Niger and Benue with a population of approximately twenty million people, which by sheer weight of numbers controls the Federal House of Representatives of Nigeria. The Northern Region is two-thirds Moslem, the rest Christian or Animist. The dominant tribes are the Hausa Negro and the ruling Fulani tribe, invaders of red-skinned Mediterranean stock.

Nigeria has a broad economic base and is a "have" nation according to African standards, being almost self-sufficient. Nigeria's economy is primarily agricultural, with individually-worked small holdings. Cooperatives for marketing and savings and loans play a large role in the economy. Nigeria has a well-distributed national income and nearly complete self-sufficiency in food. However, the economy is quite sensitive to the world demand for raw materials which it exports: tin, columbite for jet motors, cotton, and cacao. Furthermore, Nigeria is the world's largest exporter of peanuts, palm oil, and palm kernels. Nigeria needs capital to move the economy upward, especially from its present agricultural base. Coal is also being exported but there is not enough capital to develop other minerals such as iron, zinc and lead. The Niger Delta swamp discoveries of oil in 1956 may be basic in this problem of capital. Since three out of every four Nigerians are engaged in agriculture, anything which will bring about increased investment and improvement in agricultural education could easily double the wealth of Nigeria. The educational system at the present time, from elementary school through the university, tends to pull boys to the towns and cities and away from the farms. Nigeria as yet does not have an adequate soil survey and a great deal needs to be done in the realm of agricultural research. Emphasis is needed upon technological engineering and business training from stenographic work to management if Nigeria is to have the proper type of manpower. Nigeria is a case example of the need for a balanced educational system which is adapted to the needs of a developing country.

The historical development of Nigeria can be sketched as follows.

The Ife and Benin cultures reached a very high level of excellence a thousand years ago and were in contact with Mediterranean civilization. The Ife and Benin bronzes are among today's most beautiful antiquities. Later Nigeria was oriented towards the north and the trade routes of the Sahara. By the end of the fifteenth century the town of Kano was a center of both northern trade and Muslim education. The Fulani tribe invaded and conquered the Hausa kingdom of the north. In the eighteenth century the slave trade flourished on the coast of Nigeria but was abolished by the British in 1807. The British gradually penetrated from the coast into the interior, making Lagos the center of control by 1861. The colonial administrators and commissioners did much to advance the rule of law and justice in these tribal societies.

In the nineteenth century educational progress was pioneered by missionaries. Gradually the British government came to support education. The first Western education in Nigeria was literary and the civil servants and administrators were university graduates in the humanities and arts. The great symbols of prestige in Nigeria have been the literary education and the university degree; practical subjects such as technology and agriculture have not been greatly admired or esteemed. It was only in the first decade of the twentieth century that grants for education were made and the first state school was opened at Kings College at Lagos in 1909.

Nigeria has already become one of the significant culture areas of the African continent. This new African nation was recognized as a fully independent member of the British Commonwealth on October 1, 1960. Nigeria has significance not only because of its size, but also because of its present high level of progress toward democratic and disciplined self-government. In October, 1958, a parliamentary-type government was set up in Nigeria with a federal legislature of two houses: a Senate of 52 members and a House of Representatives of 320 members. The first Prime Minister of Nigeria was Alhaji Sir Abubakar Tafawa Balewa, a federal executive chosen from and answerable to the House.

Nigeria has undertaken the rapid development of an appropriate educational system. One of the most significant analyses of education and its role in advancing culture through the proper education of manpower has come from Nigeria in The Report of the Commission on the Post School Certificate and Higher Education, *Invest-*

ment in Education, (1960). *Investment in Education* drives home
the point that any ideal educational system must possess a balance
between elementary, secondary, and higher education. Each stage
of education must have the numbers of students which are appropriate for the type of culture or society which supports the educational
system. Nigeria has an imbalance at present because it is putting
as much as two-thirds of the total educational budget into elementary education, which is dangerously handicapped by the generally
low standard of teacher education. The secondary schools also
suffer from a very inadequate supply of properly educated teachers.
Recommendations to strengthen teacher training colleges have been
made since no educational system is any stronger than its teachers.
The Northern Region is particularly handicapped because some
twelve million of the Muslims inherited the ancient Koranic tradition and very few European-type schools were established in the
area. Only nine per cent of the children in the Northern Region
attend elementary schools. Only 4000 out of the two million children of secondary school age are enrolled. The Northerners who
wish to attend a university have to go to the Western Region or
overseas.

The Commission Report estimated that high-level manpower needs
in Nigeria over the next ten years would be a minimum of 80,000
people with post-secondary educational training. Nigeria's young
people are her most precious resource and investment in their education should be the first charge upon the finances of the nation.
Provision for their higher education must begin without delay:
"Modern dams, power stations, textile factories, or steel mills can
be constructed within a few years. But it takes between ten and
fifteen years to develop the managers, the administrators, and the
engineers to operate them."[1] The "educational pyramid" of Nigeria
contracts too sharply above the base to meet Nigeria's needs for
high-level manpower. The Commission pointed out that university
degrees, "like money, must have currency in other nations," and
that:

> . . . the activities of the university know no frontiers save the fron-
> tiers of knowledge . . . there is no room in the academic world for

---

[1] *Investment in Education,* p. 50.

a university which does not set itself international standards . . . high academic standards are not incompatible with relevance to national needs. But it does mean that a university has to be insulated from the hot and cold winds of politics. Responsibility for its management must be vested in an autonomous council.[2]

The Commission recommended that a National Universities Commission be set up (similar to the British University Grants Committee) with "A secure income, provided as a block grant, to be disbursed entirely at its own discretion." Their recommendations were that the Federal Government of Nigeria concentrate its resources upon the support of four universities, including two new universities in the Northern Region at Zaria and in the Federal Territory at Lagos, and on the improvement and consolidation of university facilities in the Western Region at Ibadan and in the Eastern Region at Enugu and Nsukka with priority given to the North and East. *Investment in Education* stated that: "only the teacher can lay a solid foundation for national development. Economic growth and political stability alike depend on how well he does his work. He is Nigeria's ambassador to the future, and he deserves full rights and privileges from his countrymen."[3] As in other countries, money, perquisites, and public attitude must convince the teacher that he is important to the general welfare of the nation. If teaching staffs are raided to provide personnel for other fields, all programs in a country fail. The Federal Government's three regions offer a laboratory for observation of the relationship between an educational system, educated manpower needs, and a country's future.

Nigeria and Egypt have provided valuable case examples of education in two different culture areas. Other African nations are making their unique contributions to the advancement of education. French-speaking African countries have carried out significant educational operations as have other language areas. Of paramount importance is the fact that Africa has undertaken a cooperative effort in educational strategy. The Conference of African States on the Development of Education in Africa took place in Addis Ababa in May 16–25, 1961, in accordance with the UNESCO resolution "to convene a conference of African States in 1961 with a view to

---

[2] *Ibid.*, p. 31.
[3] *Ibid.*, p. 90.

establishing an inventory of educational needs and a programme to meet those needs in the coming years, and to invite the United Nations, the other Specialized Agencies and the International Atomic Energy Agency to co-operate with UNESCO in the preparation and organization of the Conference." The Director General of UNESCO and the Executive Secretary of the United Nations Economic Commission for Africa, together with other United Nations specialized agencies, organized the conference with thirty-nine African and European governments as participants, together with observers from other governments and the representatives of ten United Nations agencies. The Conference members dealt with needs: "as revealed by the African government statements and UNESCO documents . . . spread from primary school through university and adult education levels . . . embracing all the auxiliary and related services essential to balanced programmes of education." The recommendations made were wise and far-seeing; for example, it was recommended:

1. That education, under appropriate conditions, is gainful economic investment and contributes to economic growth;

2. That the development of human resources is as urgent and essential as the development of natural resources;

3. That educational investment is of a long-term nature but, if properly planned, obtains simultaneously a high rate of return;

4. That the content of education should be related to economic needs, greater weight being given to science and its applications;

5. That in Africa, at its present level of development, the highest priority in education should be accorded to ensuring that an adequate proportion of the population receives at secondary and post-secondary levels the kinds of skills required for economic development;

6. That African countries should aim at providing universal primary education within two decades; at the same time special attention should be given to adult education and on-the-job training; . . .

Furthermore, the members of the Conference were concerned with producing more secondary graduates who would go on to the university, with increasing emphasis upon technical and agricultural education, and above all with according high priority to the training of teachers in order to improve the quality of education. In general, they emphasized that "wherever feasible an optional range of specialized courses within one institution is preferable to a variety of institutions." The Addis Ababa Conference marked a significant step forward in planning the future development of African education, and was followed up by subsequent implementation.

CHAPTER V

Education in American Culture Areas

The continents of North and South America constitute the New World, in which mankind was given opportunities to search for freedom and advance civilization. Woodrow Wilson was speaking of North America when he said: "America was created in order that every man should have the same chance as every other man to exercise mastery over his own fortunes," and Sarmiento had the same belief about South America. The nations of North and South America have been able to use the massive cultural inheritance from Europe and Asia in science, technology, government, and education to fashion new civilizations, but their rate of growth has varied. Brazil and the United States provide significant examples of the differences in development of national style and educational strategy in North and South. The United States belongs to a small group of fortunate nations whose balance of people and land resources has always been favorable and whose culture benefited from European modernization in technology, science, and education without being handicapped by the weight of a feudal or traditional society. The United States won its freedom from colonial control and began its drive toward the dynamics of mass production, an economy of abundance, and equal access to educational opportunities. Brazil had a favorable balance in natural resources and population but was handicapped by a traditional culture even after winning her freedom from colonial rule. Brazil's acceleration toward industrial growth, economic abundance, and universal education got underway only at the beginning of the twentieth century.

Brazil

The United States of Brazil is one of the giant countries of the world, with an area of approximately 3,290,000 square miles. It is almost as large as Canada, but with more than three times Canada's population. The 65 millon people of Brazil are concentrated primarily along the coastal areas. The young nation's major theme is rapid growth: it is seeking to move its frontiers of settlement inland while expanding its industrialized economy.

Brazil's huge land mass with an abundance of natural resources and a varied climate presents a challenge to education. Three of its major regions are the Amazon River Valley, the Northeast Peninsula and the Brazilian plateau. The immense State of Amazonas is covered with tropical rain-forests and its major highways are the Amazon River and its tributaries. The Northeast Peninsula is a semiarid area centered around Natal and Recife. The great Brazilian plateau of the Matto Grosso slopes eastward, falling off sharply near the sea. The major cities are concentrated along the southeastern coast from Rio de Janeiro and São Paulo toward the south. Brazil has become heavily industrialized and urbanized in these metropolitan areas in contrast to the scattered and isolated settlements of the interior. The new capital city of Brasilia has been built in the interior in order to advance settlement and develop the area.

Brazil's population is one of the racial melting pots of the world. Its people are divided into approximately sixty-two per cent whites of European origin, twenty-seven per cent mulattoes from intermarriages of whites and Negroes in the early colonial days, about ten per cent Negroes, and the remainder Mongoloid stock, native Indians, and Japanese immigrants. Brazil has a wide spectrum of European origins, including Portuguese, Spaniards, Italians, and Germans. Large German, Italian, Polish, and Japanese immigrant groups are concentrated in the states of the Southeast and South as foreign language blocs. The Federal Government in World War I took over the jurisdiction of schools and made the national language, Portuguese, mandatory for instruction. The population has tended to move in from rural areas to the southeastern urban areas producing the growth of shanty towns close to magnificent modern architecture. In general, the population distribution is seventy per cent rural and thirty per cent urban. Educationally speaking, the population pattern and the vast distances of Brazil have contributed to problems of providing adequate schools and teaching. Brazil is still a frontier area with less than two people per square mile in the majority of the states.

Brazil has been traditionally a one-crop agricultural economy shifting from sugar cane to rubber and then to coffee. The agricultural base has been broadened: Brazil now produces not only half the world's coffee but also a third of its bananas and a fifth of its cacao. The basis of the national diet is rice and beans and much of the country—especially the "polygon of drought" in the northeast—suffers from undernourishment. World War II forced Brazil further in the direction of industrialization with approximately 40,000 new factories established after the beginning of the war and in the decade following. Huge hydroelectric power developments and steel plants have been part of Brazil's growth. Minerals provide a major area of production although coal, oil, and gas fuels must be developed further in order to use more effectively the great deposits of iron, bauxite, manganese, monazite, beryllium, and nickel.

The social structure of Brazil has been changing very rapidly because of the industrial and urban shifts. Laborers on the land and in the city are being organized into unions and are able to exert legislative pressure for their advancement. The social structure is in process of change with more freedom of choice in marriage and greater opportunities for women in education and work.

The implications for educational change are obvious, underlining the need for increased agricultural, commercial, and technological education. The problem of educated manpower is fundamental to economic and social development, and Brazil is moving to meet that challenge.

The historical development of Brazilian culture and education began with the coming of the Portuguese in 1500. For over 200 years education was carried on by the Jesuits. The expulsion of the Jesuits by the Portuguese ruler Pombal in 1759 destroyed the beginnings of a pattern of education. The Empire was formed in 1822 when Brazil declared her independence from Portugal. During this period the nation drew away from Portuguese thought and moved in the direction of the French school system for a limited elite, which was encyclopedic and scholastic. At this time the primary careers for sons of the upper classes—the politicians, bureaucrats, or lords of great estates—were in medicine, law, politics, or government service. The major emphasis was upon the schools for the upper economic and social group. The Brazilian Empire divided responsibility for public schools between the provinces and the central government. The Emperors Pedro I and Pedro II attempted to create a free popular system of education but found this plan too difficult to carry out because of shortages in teachers and money, and the lack of interest on the part of the common people.

The Republic of Brazil was created in 1889. The period from 1890 to 1920 was one of slow exploration in educational orientation and structure. Primary education lagged in development despite the efforts of Vaz and Campos. The federal government only aided primary education when it was faced with the problem of nationalizing its wide variety of settlers. The reform movement in education was started after World War I under the leadership of such men as Filho, Teixeira, and Azevedo. There was a strong reaction against the traditional scholastic system as part of the general Brazilian unrest, which came to a head in the Revolution of 1930 when Vargas took over the presidency. The Revolution of 1930 demonstrated the rapid growth potential of Brazil. Migrations took place within Brazil with a centering of population around São Paulo. There was heavy immigration from overseas and ideas from North America and Europe had an increasing impact upon Brazilian institutions. Industrialization accelerated and brought about a new social mobility. Under the influence of the recently gained democracy, education was given a democratic social function and the curriculum was enriched. John Dewey's stirring words were used in the statement of aims: "The panorama of an ampler and richer life for man in general, a life of greater freedom and equal opportunity for all, to the end that each may develop and achieve all that is in him to be." The reform movement of the 1930's brought about the first public school system which was designed to educate all of Brazil's children.

Brazil has had to struggle with the inheritance of the past which emphasized scholastic academic training for a few in the direction of a limited number of learned professions and with failure to educate the masses of people for competence in agriculture, technology and citizenship. A major problem was the rigid selectivity for the universities enforced in secondary and even primary schools. The basis of selectivity was an academic set of requirements with an almost impossibly wide series of scholastic subjects designed for further academic training leading to the universities. The basic document for education in Brazil is the constitution of 1946. The various states assume responsibility for their own systems of education, whereas the federal government retains primary responsibility for maintaining national norms and remedying local deficiencies.

Private schools have played a significant role in Brazilian education. These schools, founded mainly by religious organizations, are inspected and controlled by the federal government. The Ministry of Education and Culture was organized in 1953, to strengthen uniform educational policies on a nationwide basis. A National Institute of Educational Research had been organized in 1937 as a research foundation under the Ministry of Education and Culture with the educators Filho, Carvalho, and Teixeira playing a major role in its operation. Its functions were to distribute federal funds to elementary and secondary schools, to direct the school-building program, and to conduct research. With the foundation of the Brazilian Center of Educational Research in 1955 the research functions of INEP were expanded and basic studies on Brazilian life have been carried out and communicated to the teachers of Brazil.

Brazil has come a long distance in her fight against illiteracy. The first national census in 1920 showed that seventy-five per cent of the adults were illiterate and thirty-five per cent of school age children were in school. The progress of educational reform reduced illiteracy to approximately sixty per cent in 1940 and to fifty per cent in 1950. The primary school provides for the children between seven and twelve years of age. The rural areas tend to keep to the traditional four-year curriculum and school "evasion" has been high because of lack of accommodation, inefficiently trained teachers, and rigid curricula. Brazilian schools, beginning with the elementary level, are still quite selective although they are opening their doors wider and broadening curricula.

The secondary educational system has been closely related to its original European base with an emphasis upon the *ginasio* and *collejio* (lower- and upper-secondary schools) which offer college-preparatory programs of education. These academic secondary schools are greatly esteemed and traditionally lead to higher social status and financial reward by way of the university. The other types of secondary schools—industrial, commercial, agricultural and normal—have had a much smaller enrollment and yet it is in these areas that instruction should be expanded. The contemporary pressures of organized labor, industrial and urban growth, and the wider social and economic range of pupils have had an impact upon the role of the secondary school. Trends have formed toward modernization of curricula and teaching in order to cope with the rapid growth pattern in Brazilian life. Transfer between the various types of secondary education has been made easier. Graduates of industrial and commercial schools can now choose college careers. The twenty-one universities of Brazil are engaged in a process of expansion, many of them in the direction of the university city formula. The entire university system is only thirty years old. Previously higher education was limited to the professional schools of medicine and law and engineering. The first modern university was organized in 1920 as the University of Rio de Janeiro, combining the Law School, the Medical School and the Polytechnic School of Rio de Janeiro. The Statute of Brazilian Universities of 1931 set the pattern of university organization with a requirement for at least three faculties of higher education including a faculty of philosophy, sciences or letters and any two of law, medicine, or engineering.

Brazil, with its expanding frontier of settlement, its growing urbanization and industrialization, and its population expansion, in a varied continental expanse presents one of the critical educational undertakings of the world. The reform movement of the 1930's has provided a strong educational base which, with adequate research and cooperation between federal and state governments, can enable Brazil to advance. Brazil faces the challenge of accelerated investment in education in order to create sufficient high-level manpower to cope with her rapid growth pattern.

Other Latin American countries have carried out their own revolutions in cultural growth, using education as a primary instrument. The Revolution of 1910 in Mexico used the rallying cry: *"Educar es redimir"* ("To educate is to redeem"); and Mexico went on to create her modern culture through the process of education. The rise of education was slow at first in Latin America but advanced more rapidly after the revolutions for independence under the leadership of such gifted men as Domingo Faustino Sarmiento in Argentina and Chile. But the real transformations in Latin American education began to gather speed only in the mid-twentieth century.

The United States

The land, people, and culture of the United States have been elements in a vast acculturation in which the rich inheritances of many of the world's civilizations have found a new synthesis. The continental area of the United States stretches in a wide band across North America from the Atlantic to the Pacific Oceans, with climate ranging from Arctic cold to tropical warmth. The fifty states comprise some 3,615,000 square miles. The American population, a majestic mingling of races and cultures, numbered over 180 million in 1960. This five per cent of the world's population produces approximately forty per cent of the world's industrial goods. Wyndham Lewis believed that the amalgamation of many ethnic groups in the United States and the invention of new patterns of living would perhaps provide the beginnings of "cosmic man." Americans have their cultural roots in Europe and Asia, in Africa and Latin America but they have also developed novel indigenous traits. Three outstanding American traits are *idealism, mobility,* and *productivity*. The revolutionary nature of American development and its distinctive national style of life and education have foundations in these traits.

American mobility has been both geographical and cultural. The westward movement of the frontier of settlement, the booming growth of cities, the far voyaging of whalers, clippers, jet planes and space rockets, and the automobile-centered tempo of life are aspects of this geographical mobility. Cultural mobility has been demonstrated in the use of universal education as an instrument of self-improvement and social advance. The young could play an important role earlier than the traditional civilizations permitted. Everyone acquired a greater chance to determine his own future. American productivity has involved an unusual combination of scientific experimentation and technological innovation to create an economy of abundance and an affluent society. Such productivity required an acceleration in quality and quantity of education to create the high-level manpower needed for research, management and operation. "The Continuing American Revolution" was based above all upon an evolving idealism, transcendental and utilitarian, which provided a humanitarian orientation. The Christian, Hebraic and Hellenic ethical traditions were carried forward by the Americans in the New World in novel indigenous patterns. The triad of ethical ideals, economic productivity, and cultural mobility in the broadest sense were the catalysts in "The Continuing American Revolution."

The history of cultural and educational change in the United States may be divided into three major periods. The first or Dawn

Period, in the seventeenth and eighteenth centuries, was characterized by a transplanted elite-mass education from Europe with a gradual change around the end of the eighteenth century toward a dawning universal education. The tempo of the times was slow: movement by ox-cart, horse, and canoe was not over seven miles per hour. Family units were almost self-sufficient, and the handicraft technology used water, wind, and muscle for power. Schools had a strong religious base: Episcopal, Congregational, Dutch Reformed, or Presbyterian. The apprentice system provided both literacy and training in a craft. The American Revolution was social, economic, and political, creating a new nation free to set a course unchecked by the traditional class structure, political conservatism, and economic obstacles of the Old World. Toward the end of the period a distinctly American strategy of education began to take shape. The district or community elementary school developed in New England. The beginnings of the American high school, which was to supersede the Latin grammar school, appeared in Benjamin Franklin's *Proposals* (1749) for an academy with a realistic curriculum. The American four-year arts college developed as a residential college with courses in the classics and natural philosophy and produced such leaders as Jefferson, Madison, and John Adams.

The second or Formative Period, in the nineteenth century, witnessed the accelerating growth of an indigenous American culture. A fundamental technological shift came with the application of the steam engine to manufacturing, mining, and transportation in a system of mass production. The frontiers of settlement first lumbered, then raced westward across the continent with the aid of new power tools and the mass production of the steel plow, wire fence, windmill, repeating rifles, and six-shooters. At the same time, the steam engine was adapted to factory, railroad, and river boat, and created great agglomerations of population around merchandising, factory, and transport centers. The teachers in the growing system of indigenous universal education helped to weld together many different cultures. An American system of universal education was gradually formed, with an eight-year elementary school, a four-year high school, and a four-year college or university. Noah Webster helped to build up American education with his *Blueback Speller* and his scholarly and original *Dictionary*. Ralph Waldo Emerson founded the American philosophy of transcendental idealism and led the way toward intellectual independence in his Phi Beta Kappa Address of 1837, *The American Scholar,* insisting that Americans break away from their imitation of Europe. Horace Mann led the fight for "universal" rather than "partial" education, *i.e.,* extending education into adolescence beyond the fourteenth year. The Morrill Act of 1862 founded the land grant colleges to meet the demands of agriculture and engineering. The Civil War devastated the South and delayed its economic and educational advance. By the end of this period the modern American university had been developed with its graduate and professional colleges, its laboratories and libraries and research institutes. The universities became a center for the scientific study of the problems of American civilization and a major force in its theoretical and actual construction. The pattern of informal education grew rapidly with the coming of the daily newspaper, low-price periodicals, large-scale book publishing, and the foundation of libraries, art galleries, and museums.

The third or Period of Mid-Passage, in the twentieth century, began with another great shift in American life. The frontier of settlement as a line of advance westward had disappeared and the country became increasingly urban and industrial. The United States came of age in literature, the arts, economics, government, technology, and education and found itself involved in international diplomacy as a major power. Technologically speaking, the United States moved into new industrial revolutions, characterized not only by new power sources—petroleum, electric, atomic, and solar—but also by the creation of electronic equivalents to the human nervous system such as automatic computers. Large scale scientific research linked higher education and industrial, communication, transportation, and mercantile organizations together with the federal government.

The development of universal education as an instrument in cultural change continued despite two world wars and a major economic depression. G. Stanley Hall, the psychologist, founded the child study movement and emphasized the process of evolutionary growth. William James was a founder of pragmatism and spoke for a pluralistic approach. John Dewey's influence pervaded American education and culture. He reflected the American frontiersman's optimism and democracy and insisted that the school should be part of society linked to life with an activity curriculum. Dewey's great book, *Democracy and Education,* defined philosophy as the theory of education in its broadest sense and balanced the value of subject-matter areas with the growth and development of the individual. The American educators pioneered in the world movement toward the expansion of universal education, developing a 6-3-3-4 system of education with elementary school, junior, and senior high school, and higher education. Junior high schools and junior colleges improved the continuity of education. By the close of World War I, the American comprehensive high school assumed its form, putting four general courses of study—academic or college preparatory, technical, vocational, and homemaking—under one roof. The growth of the consolidated school making use of school buses enabled country districts to combine single-room, single-teacher schools into large administrative units so that both elementary and secondary grades benefitted from laboratories, workshops, and libraries, and better organized curriculum. The Great Depression and World War II involved the United States more and more deeply in the international changes in education through United Nation agencies, UNESCO and Point Four Plans. Soldiers carried new ideas in their knapsacks from continent to continent and came home to accelerate the extension of universal education into the higher education level under the G.I. Bill. The conflict with totalitarian ideology continued after World War II and forced the United States to re-examine her national style and strategy of education.

This process of historical change resulted in the formation of an educational system with certain basic characteristics. American education is universal throughout elementary, secondary, and higher education. Both sexes study together at every stage of education. The significance of coeducation has been extensive in the culture pattern and has had constructive results in opening up opportunities for women and educating men more realistically and aesthetically. The American comprehensive high school produces both amateurs and experts, giving a general education to all but recognizing that each individual has particular talents which must be identified and sought out.

Each of the fifty states controls its own system of education instead of being directed by a central ministry. There is local community responsibility through school boards made up of elected citizens. However, federal influence upon education has been extensive, including the Morrill Act of 1862 and the Smith-Hughes Act of 1917. The U. S. Office of Education has made noteworthy contributions to the advancement of the educational system. Students learn democratic living in schools which are miniatures of the democratic society of the nation. Toward this end a pattern of extracurricular activities has been developed, including student government, varsity and intramural sports, bands, orchestras, choruses, and dramatic and debating societies. The system of public education is secular since church and State are separated in the United States. The American strategy of education has evolved into a slowly accelerated general education which specializes gradually and relatively late on the collegiate or higher education level. Controversies have been vigorous concerning the balance between "life adjustment" and "subject-matter centered" curricula, liberal education and professional specialization, federal and state control of education. The United States has had to cope with the problems of adequate education for minority groups, segregation, attempts to secure federal financial support for sectarian schools, and educational inequalities between various states. The public education system of the United States from elementary school to university is strengthened by private education providing essential opportunities for experimentation and variety.

Higher education in the United States has been characterized by the following trends: a continuing acculturation with its original European base in higher education, the growth of an indigenous and original pattern of higher education, the building up of diversity of patterns of both public and private higher education, the pursuit of ultimate truth in all fields of knowledge by scholars in various disciplines, and a continuing professional impact upon a dynamic technological and humanistic culture.

Some analysts have charged that there is a discontinuity between United States undergraduate education, mainly English in background, and graduate education, mainly Continental in its traditions. Actually, however, the first two years of undergraduate education provide a transition into a systematic exploration of knowledge and upper classmen are already writing research papers which link into graduate work. The American two-year junior college provides a transition to the last two years of the university.

The United States has built up an indigenous structure of higher education. The four-year arts college is an American invention (as Richard Hofstadter, C. DeWitt Hardy, and others have pointed out) and had a true balance between the arts and sciences from the earliest days (eighteenth century Harvard had one major professor teaching natural philosophy or science and the other teaching philosophy and logic and languages). Furthermore, the creation of the land grant college or university broadened the curriculum so that United States higher education often combines on the same campus the ancient faculties of arts and science, medicine, and law with the newer faculties of agriculture, engineering, education, and business administration. The universities in the United States have from the beginning engaged in a pursuit of ultimate truth in every field of knowledge and the impact of university thinking has had a far-reaching effect in every aspect of the American civilization, as Merle Curti has demonstrated in his admirable book, *The Growth of American Thought*. The strength of American universal education lies in its balance of unity and diversity; and as James Bryant Conant puts it: "equality of opportunity for all youth, equality of respect for all honest citizens," as goals for American education.[1]

The United States' strategy of education has also been enriched by its bonds with certain other young members of the English-speaking world and their contributions to the advancement of education, namely, Canada, Australia, and New Zealand. Each of these countries has devoted great intelligence, treasure and effort to the progress of universal education and has played a major role in the Pacific and Atlantic community of nations.

[1] J. B. Conant, *The Citadel of Learning* (New Haven: Yale University Press, 1956), pp. 23ff.

CHAPTER VI

Developmental Trends in
Components of Educational Systems

Orientation

The eminent American biologist, Edwin Grant Conklin, said: "We are today only children in the morning of time and before us lie the countless centuries and millennia of man's vast future." Especially in a nuclear age it would seem that every civilization must pursue excellence in its educational system as the best guarantee of its own survival and progress. A nation must engage in the intelligent improvement of all the major components of its educational system in order to attain excellence. These components may be grouped into three major categories: *orientation,* including philosophy, law, finance; *organization,* including general structure, pre-elementary, elementary, secondary and higher education, and mass media; *operation,* including students, teachers, curricula, methods of instruction, instructional materials, evaluation and testing, guidance, supervision, and administration. The orientation of a nation or culture is essential in determining the success of its educational system. Abraham Lincoln was thinking of this when he said: "If we could just know where we are and whither we are tending, we could better judge what to do and how to do it." Orientation includes the philosophical world picture controlling the aims and objectives of its pattern of education. Legal statutes and financial budgets are tangible expressions and implementations of the national philosophy for an educational system.

Law is the safest shield, *tutissima cassis,* as Edward Coke, the great recorder and interpreter of the English Common law, pointed out. Throughout the world statutes and legal codes have spelled out the trends in orientation of education. The codes of the 1860's and 1870's in the United States, England, France, and Japan showed trends toward a philosophy of rapid extension of free, compulsory public elementary education and a beginning expansion of secondary and higher education. Many twentieth century statutes have recorded "a ground swell" toward secondary education for all as in England's Butler Act of 1944 and France's Langevin Act of 1947. The laws have also faithfully recorded the struggle between the proponents of generalized study of basic academic subjects and the proponents of more specialized vocational knowledge and skills. The Soviet laws of 1958–59 emphasized increased polytechnization and learning in vocational areas while the U. S. National Defense Education Act of the same period expanded the teaching of such fundamental subjects as modern languages, mathematics, science, and guidance. Laws are directly linked with financial budgets and inadequate appropriations cannot implement the philosophy behind the law.

Accordingly, a national philosophy of education is indicated not only in official government statements or in statutes or laws which implement these statements, but also in the actual expenditures for education. Because of the varying definitions of educational expenditures, it is difficult to make international comparisons of percentages of national income spent on education, which range from one to plus seven or eight per cent. Originally, expenditures for the improvement of education were estimated on the basis of faith; now we possess statistical proof. Historically speaking, Japan and Denmark represent countries which lacked natural resources but attained a higher and earlier rate of growth than much richer neighboring countries. Denmark's folk high schools, founded by Bishop Grundtvig and his associates, together with the excellent base of compulsory elementary education, enabled Danish farmers to understand and to carry out extensive changes in their productive activity and laid a basis of continued prosperity for Denmark. The Danes replaced grain production with intensive dairy farming, importing grain from the competitive farm lands of the New World. In Japan the fundamental factor in rapid economic growth was the establishment of public compulsory elementary education in the Meiji era, which practically eliminated illiteracy by the closing years of the nineteenth century. On the other hand, China and India, richer in natural resources, were burdened with a high rate of illiteracy and a low scale of economic development. Pioneer research undertaken by Professors Schultz, Lewis, Solow, Becker,

Edding, Vaisey, Kairov, and Lobel has given us firm statistical data on the economic importance of education in the progress of nations. For example, Profesesor Solow—after examination of the aggregate farm production in the United States between 1900 and 1960— came to the conclusion that only ten per cent of the economic growth could be accounted for by capital accumulation, new physical resources and population growth, so that the remaining ninety per cent was due to residual factors under the general heading of technological progress, which included education, organization, and inventiveness. The estimates of the economists concerning returns from investment in education were very striking. Professor Becker of the United States made careful estimates for the National Bureau of Economic Research, indicating that in 1950 the male population of the United States earned 14.8 per cent return on what they had as private individuals invested in high school, college, and university education—including both their own direct costs and their earnings lost while receiving an education. If the public costs were added, the rate was reduced to eleven per cent. In the Soviet Union, Professor Kairov calculated that the introduction of universal four-year education resulted in a benefit to the economy forty-three times the original sum expended upon it. These figures were for a society with a highly developed education and a high level of economic growth.

Orientation of educational systems is based upon philosophy above all. Philosophy has in general five areas of problems, each of which is investigated by a major branch of philosophy. These branches and their problems are directly related to problems faced in education:

PHILOSOPHY	EDUCATION
Axiology: Theory of values, ethics, and aesthetics.	The general aims and objectives of a system of education.
Metaphysics: The nature of man and the universe.	The nature of human beings and their cultural surroundings, teachers and students.
Epistemology: The theory of knowledge.	The areas of knowledge or subject matter and curricula.
Logic: The art of critical thinking.	Methods of instruction.
Politics, or Philosophy of Administration: Philosophy of a specific area of knowledge or profession.	Administration, personnel, public relations, in the realm of education.

The great branches of philosophy are in many ways parallel to and helpful in solving not only the major problems of philosophy but also the major problems of education. Each branch of philosophy not only has a direct and parallel relationship to a major problem faced in education but also can be very effective in assisting other branches of philosophy in the solution of major problems of education. Logic is not only directly concerned with methods of instruction and teaching but also with the clarification and delineation of general aims and objectives in a system of education and in general provides invaluable critiques of theories and practices in other areas of education.

The philosophy or orientation of a culture's educational system concerns itself with the type of person or social character it desires to form or produce. Madariaga has suggested that the English admire men of action; the French, men of intellect; the Spanish, men of passion. David Riesman and his associates argued in *The Lonely Crowd* that individuals and cultures have historically tended to pursue three types of social character; the tradition-directed, the inner-directed, and the other-directed types. Riesman said that in the West the Renaissance and Reformation produced a shift from a tradition-directed society to an inner-directed society which secured conformity by implanting competitive goals very early in an individual's life and substituted a self-governing psychological gyroscope for the taboos and penalties imposed from without in the tradition-directed societies of the past. The other-directed society in which individuals are controlled by a radar-like sensitivity to their peer groups is pictured as appearing with the growth of industrialism, capitalism, and urbanization especially in the metropolises of the United States and, to some extent, in Europe. These analysts felt that Communism has become a dangerous, reactionary, and menacing force in the world arena because it is attempting to arrange the future of the world according to images of the past such as the class struggle, the victory of the proletariat, and the use of force and conformity to engage in the destructive struggle for survival rather than engaging in the mutual aid and constructive interchange of technology, education, and economics, so essential to constructive acculturation.

Each culture or civilization seeks a philosophical ideal or utopia through use of an educational system which is structured to produce such a future. Gardner Murphy has suggested we are now engaged in a search for human potentialities on a higher level than ever before. Democracy provides the soil of freedom which encourages diversity and the development of a wide range of individual talents while totalitarianism insists upon a deadly uniformity in the culture's world picture.

The future of the world is going to be determined by conflict or cooperation between masses of people. Those masses will be successful which clearly understand the orientation of their educational system toward a philosophical world picture and who structure and organize and operate their educational system to attain these goals. We cannot afford to live in a time of disenchantment and of pessimism in which man is mainly concerned with the means of production and with a mechanical approach to the future possibilities of his environment. Ernst Cassirer and Julian Huxley have pointed out that the uniqueness of man lies in his ability to create new dimensions of reality through his capacity for symbolic conceptual thought. Man lives in a symbolic universe which enables him continually to change his physical environment with new instruments of power created by his own ideas. Man can create utopias or constructs of symbols and ideas which transcend a passive agreement with the present state of affairs, help overcome his natural inertia, and give him the god-like ability to create a nobler universe. The universities of the world today are examples of humanity's use of an educational invention not only to transmit the cultural inheritance of the past and to operate the powerful engines and theories of the present but also to picture a wider range of rewarding futures. A type of utopia with which every scholar, statesman, teacher, student must increasingly be concerned is one with an "ethical ecology" —an environment characterized by mutual aid, which has an ethical orientation providing a good life for all participants. This utopian construct insists that no organism or society of organisms or culture can afford to degrade or deface its own environment since this leads to self-destruction; rather, the organism or society must preserve and enrich its surroundings toward a climax type of balance.

Organization

The organization of a national educational system mirrors the philosophy which undergirds and orients its civilization. The structural formulae are derived from the past and affected by the pressures of contemporary changes and of the developing future. The past is very persistent and enduring in its effect. The structure of modern education has been derived from such different sources as the Reformation vernacular elementary school, the Latin grammar secondary school and the medieval university, with consequent lack of continuity and articulation. As we have seen in the study of the educational systems of various culture areas, the indigenous history of the civilization has a definite effect on the shaping of the structure. The general structure of education has differing relationships to the chronological ages of the children and the major periods of infancy, childhood, adolescence, and adulthood.

Some primary organizational differences should be underlined. The classic elite-mass system of education has a common elementary or primary school. A few, at age eleven or twelve, are allowed to continue in special secondary schools leading to the university and professional schools. The rest of the school population pursues a continuation of the elementary school which terminates formally at fourteen or fifteen years of age. Under the elite system, about three to five per cent of the age group go into higher education. The universal system of education includes all of the school population in common elementary and secondary schools which hold the majority of the school population, despite some drop-outs, until age sixteen to eighteen. Approximatetly ten to twenty per cent continue their studies in some institution of higher education.

Provision for continuity between the various stages of education is an important characteristic in an educational system. In Russia the emphasis is placed upon a ten-year school system. Within this continuity are divisions at the secondary level into various types of schools such as vocational technicums and newer polytechnic schools. In the European school structure, there are breaks in articulation between elementary and secondary education which have been attacked in various ways. The German *Rahmenplan* uses extensions of the *Grundschule* through additional grades to gain continuity. The French have employed *cours complémentaires* to provide further articulation between the *école communale* and the *lycée*. The United States provides for continuity by making the last grade of the elementary school a bridge over into the more specialized subject-matter instruction of the junior high schools. The junior high provides a transition into the similar but more highly developed senior high school. The junior college and the first two years of the four-year college are increasingly organized to provide a better transition into the different tempo and demands of university work.

The structuring of an educational system so that there is segregation by the sexes is generally the case in Europe and Asia. Co-education is generally the rule in the United States. The educational system's policy with regard to "streaming," or homogenous grouping according to ability is another aspect of structure. England uses "streaming" very effectively. The evolution of school and educational buildings themselves reflects the organization of education, although splendid modern teaching is done in ancient structures. A trend has developed toward campus patterns of organization with buildings grouped on sufficient ground space to provide for open air sports and outdoor laboratory work, further expanded by transportation facilities to make more extensive use of the community and regional opportunities for education.

Pre-elementary education has been made a regular part of the school structure in France with the *école maternelle* for two- to five-year-olds. Russia has built up an extensive pre-elementary structure. Generally speaking, the preschool and kindergarten structure has lagged behind the succeeding stages of the school system. The internal organization of elementary education differs greatly in various cultures. In many countries the traditional elementary school organization is that of grades subdivided into one-room classes or forms, each carrying out its own day's work centered around books, blackboards, and notebooks. In contrast, a more flexible elementary structure involves movement from the home-room working area to other facilities: the gymnasium, library, laboratories, art rooms, studios, playing fields, and gardens.

The organization of secondary education is in a process of flux. Countries are in the midst of a controversy concerning the retention of the older specialized types of secondary schools with close correlation between social class and type of school and the newer trend toward schools of high quality which are equally accessible to all children. England may well retain a variety of secondary schools— grammar, technical, comprehensive, and modern—with enrichment of all types so as to give equally high standards of education. France and Germany are making their own carefully considered changes. The coming of modern industrial urbanized society made it increasingly unwise to retain separate secondary educational systems for different social classes because the need for well-educated human beings increased and could not be filled from the limited numbers of privileged groups. After World War II, major shifts began to take place in the direction of compulsory free secondary education through the sixteenth year and beyond. Europeans claimed that scholarships and various types of financial aid always gave the most talented an equal opportunity no matter what their background, but statistical surveys did not substantiate this view since there were too few places for all the available talent.

The changes in secondary educational organization have included several phases. The special preparatory elementary schools controlled by secondary education were generally abolished. The school-leaving age was raised from twelve to fourteen, fifteen, or sixteen years so that all children could enjoy the benefits of secondary education on an equal footing in accordance with their age, aptitude and ability. The setting up of consolidated or modern schools for rural children helped equalize opportunities. In the more highly developed and mature countries, the trend was to delay the choice of a vocation which previously had to be made at eleven or twelve years of age to sixteen years or later. In underdeveloped countries, secondary education is the most critical stage in organization because enough places must be provided for every talented student in order to provide sufficient recruits for higher education which produces the highly trained, professional, technical manpower essential to the country's advancement.

The organization of higher education is different in various cultures of the world today. In general, continental Europe has a highly selective system of higher education which is actually a series of graduate professional schools. Universities follow the model of the University of Paris with the great faculties of the arts and sciences, law, medicine, and theology. The technical, engineering, educational, and applied areas are separate from the universities as in the *grandes écoles* of France and the *Technische Hochschulen* of Germany and Switzerland. A unique characteristic of the older English university was the combination of general intellectual training provided by the university lecture halls and laboratories with the separate residential colleges of the university which emphasized the tutoring of the individual not only as a scholar but as a gentleman.

In the United States, the universities are less selective and begin with general undergraduate education. The universities also became comprehensive, including on the same campus not only the traditional faculties but also the special schools of architecture, business administration, education, and engineering. Some specialized technical schools continue but the trend is toward the more generalized and comprehensive university. The universities are the most effective organization yet devised for creating the high-level intellectual manpower essential to the solution of a wide range of problems caused by the long-range factors which shape any civilization and its education. Only the university has sufficient intellectual breadth, depth, and continuity to provide the scholars, students, working areas, libraries, and laboratories which are essential to the ongoing processes of teaching, research, and service. The university is the peak of the educational pyramid and its graduates can very rapidly affect their surroundings by their intellectual contributions. The relative growth of university populations in totalitarian nations and in democratic nations will do much to determine the outcome of the struggle for power.

Operation

The actual operation of an educational system in a country is a valuable and accurate index to its effectiveness in coping with the paramount issues of civilization. Orientation and organization may be admirable but they depend upon daily implementation in the operational sequence involving teachers, curricula and syllabi, methods of instruction and instructional materials, evaluation and testing, guidance, and administration. The status of the teacher and the level of teacher education in a country is a primary key to the effectiveness of operation. Differentiation in levels of training and pay between elementary, secondary, and higher education teachers continue to persist in many countries. Countertrends have appeared toward the equalization of status between elementary and secondary school teachers through the institution of equivalent training and pay scales. Teacher education takes place increasingly in connection with universities or colleges so as to take advantage of the basic disciplines in addition to the professional discipline of education. Curriculum-building has moved in the direction of a synthesis of broad cultural education and of specialized vocational training. Alfred North Whitehead spoke for a synthesis of the amateur and the expert in a nonbookish but aesthetic education. A French official statement of 1956 was concerned with the extension of the opportunity for *culture générale* to larger numbers of the adolescent population. The Report of the Commission on Post School Certificate and Higher Education in Nigeria (1960) stated the importance of a new type of secondary and higher education which was a synthesis between the traditional literary education and the newer education in technology, agriculture, and practical subjects.

Each educational system has made definite contributions to methods of instruction. The English have perfected tutoring, especially in the ancient universities of Oxford and Cambridge. This is an expensive and worthwhile method which has been adapted to larger groups in such systems as the preceptorial. The Germans advanced the seminar and laboratory methods of teaching in which the student learned how to carry out original research. The valuable French method of *explication de texte* examined a particular statement or thesis from every possible point of view in order to illuminate its significance. John Dewey made one of the most notable and unique American contributions to education in his problem method. He believed that teachers should use children's propensities toward action both in clarifying understanding and in motivating learning. Dewey's *How We Think* epitomizes his problem method (in reality the method of scientific thought) in the famous five steps for the student: (1) Sensing a problem, preferably one which blocks the continuity of his activity; (2) Defining the problem; (3) Obtaining data for the purpose of suggesting possible reconstructions of his activity; (4) Reasoning out implications of these suggestions; (5) Testing the most likely suggestion or theory for achieving his ends by taking action on it.

In other words the pedagogy of activity is to learn truth by testing it. Dewey advised the teacher to motivate studies by making them instrumental to the pupil's realization of his own natural proclivities.

The efficiency of teaching methods has been closely linked with improvements in instructional materials. Various cultures have made their contributions toward an educational technology by improving their materials of instruction. The English were pioneers in the production of the documentary film; the French and Germans were leaders in the production of fine maps and atlases essential to study in a wide series of disciplines; the Americans made systematic improvements in libraries through the Dewey decimal system and the general development of library science. Extensive work has been done in the audio-visual field including 16mm safety film, overhead projectors, and the use of radio and television as effective and dynamic extensions of instruction. Teaching machines of various types were devised by Pressey, Skinner, and others, and hold promise of creating an educational technology which will enable the individual student to progress at his own speed. Meanwhile the teacher can be freed for creative supervision of study but must have greater time allotted for programming of units of study in an area of knowledge. Teaching machines enable the student to solve problems programmed in sequences of increasing difficulty; correcting his own mistakes and acting as a self-tutor. The devices range from books designed for problem-solving by cross-reference rather than reading in sequence to complex electronic consoles capable of tutoring the student in history, mathematics, or contract bridge. The new educational technology can give greater efficiency and creativity to both student and teacher. Intellectual ingenuity in the employment of utilitarian power machines can create a new aesthetic excellence in teaching.

Evaluation, testing, and guidance have varied widely from country to country. The Europeans tended to emphasize oral examination and the written essay. The Americans have developed statistically controlled standardized tests and used them extensively. A sophisticated combination of testing procedures is increasingly the trend with a critical eye turned upon the weaknesses and strengths of each procedure. Testing and evaluation procedures are critical instruments because they determine the thresholds of selection at stages of the educational process. Guidance has become increasingly important as the needs, aptitudes, and abilities of students have assumed their proper role in the design of education. For example, the French reform in the Order and Decree of January 6, 1959, had the essential purpose of establishing educational guidance securely alongside actual teaching.

Administration and its allied areas of inspection and supervision are of paramount importance in the success of an educational system. Administrative policies in the relatively decentralized American system are different from those of the highly centralized French system of administration. The British system gives a high level of authority to the individual headmaster and school faculty, which is balanced by the considerable control exerted by the Ministry of Education. Sir Graham Belfort stated that educational administration should enable "the right pupils to receive the right education from the right teachers at a cost within the means of the state under conditions which will enable the pupils to profit by their training." Administration varies from country to country because definitions of what constitutes the "right" education differ materially. European headmasters and university administrators continue to teach. In the United States, administrators find it most difficult to continue any instructional activity. Administration in an educational system is concerned with the entire span of operation, personnel, budgets, organization, public relations, buildings, curriculum, and instruction and can be overwhelmed by paper work. Good administration has increasingly concerned itself with the functional improvement of instruction and the provision of an atmosphere in which teachers and students can work as a community of scholars properly protected from the many pressure groups and self-appointed critics of educational operation.

In many countries educational administrators and leaders have made statesmanlike contributions: Humayun Kabir in India, Geoffrey Crowther and M.V.C. Jeffreys in England, Roger Gal and Louis Cros in France, James Bryant Conant in the United States.

The comparative study of components of educational systems indicates a valuable cultural diversity in constructive trends which are taking place in the categories of orientation, organization, and operation despite many stubborn and persistent obstacles.

CHAPTER VII

Paramount Issues Challenging Educational Systems

What paramount issues must educational systems cope with in order to maintain and advance a national style adequate for survival and progress? The preceding investigations of education in various culture areas narrated some aspects of evolution in national styles in conjunction with analysis of components of their educational systems. It is not enough to compare the components of educational systems with regard to orientation, organization, and operation. One must also ask: How well do these components in their integrated form or *gestalt* enable nations to solve the paramount issues perennially raised by the operation of the long-range factors making up the various sectors of the nation's culture?

National Style and Acculturation

A national style is the pattern of performance which a civilization shows in coping with the paramount issues of its times. It operates in all of the areas of living which we have defined as long-range factors. The manner in which a nation's people produce technological innovations, carry out their family obligations, enjoy the arts, and conduct their governmental affairs constitutes its national style. A national pattern of performance must develop in such a way that it may advance constructive indigenous growth within and a favorable external environment without, *i.e.*, engage in a constructive process of acculturation. Melville Herskovits and his colleagues in the field of anthropology have developed the contemporary scientific use of the term *acculturation*.

Acculturation is the process of culture contact and is an integral part of the rise and development of civilization. Peoples continually meet and exchange ideas and artifacts along the trade routes, on frontiers of settlement, political boundaries, battlefields, and in international conferences. Both the United States and Japan provide examples of extensive acculturation. The United States built up its civilization from a transplantation of a wide range of European, African, and Asiatic cultures and a series of indigenous innovations. Japan brought in and adapted certain dimensions of the Tang culture of the eighth century and then many aspects of European and American cultures of the nineteenth century. These were vast educational dramas in which education may be regarded as the transit of civilization through a process of acculturation. A civilization needs insight into the close relationship between its national style and acculturation, preserving and reconstructing its own indigenous civilization while advancing its national interest in the external world environment. Such insight enables a nation to use its educational system in coping more intelligently with paramount issues. G. Hausmann calls this "The Century of Acculturation."

Educational systems must conserve their past indigenous culture, otherwise there is no basic communication, cooperation, or security. Educational organizations must be innovators coping with the pressures of the accelerating present and future. Looking at human history, one witnesses the disintegration of civilizations unable to use education as an instrument of conservation and innovation, and the continuity of civilizations which have proved able to use their educational systems to meet the challenges of paramount issues in their times. How may one examine these challenges systematically? One method is to analyze the long-range factors in culture as they relate to certain perennial issues. These issues have been cast in the old Greek form of antitheses with a zone of tension between them:

Long-Range Factors	Paramount Issues
I	
Folk	Quantity and quality
Space	Mutual aid and struggle for existence
Time	Indigenous growth and external exchange
II	
Language	Communication and imagination
Art	Aesthetics and utility
Philosophy	Adventure and peace
Religion	Ethics and faith

                    III

Social structure   Elite and mass
Government   Freedom and discipline
Economics   Innovation and conservatism

                    IV

Technology   Adaptation and creativity
Science   Natural sciences and human sciences
Health   Physique and intellect
Education   Specialization and generalization

Obviously each issue is not correlated with only one long-range factor, but in a very real sense with all of them. For the purpose of
examination, each has been linked specifically to one long-range
factor in which basic disciplines conduct research.

Folk, Space, and Time

The long-range factor of folk or population presents every nation
with the challenge of balancing quantity and quality. Nations are
presently faced with a population growth or explosion which may
outrun technological capacity to produce food, shelter, and services.
India and Japan are engaged in national programs of education in
birth control with the outcome still far from clear. Before World
War II, the United States and France seemed to be on the road to a
stabilization of population. After 1940, however, the United States
had a remarkable rise in its birthrate. A similar phenomenon occurred in France, but in both countries the margin in land and
technology was sufficient to accommodate this change. A culture
requires the education of experts in medical and social services adequate for dealing with the problem of population. The general level
of education must be high enough to utilize all the talents in the
population without waste and to facilitate rapid understanding of
the shifts in population problems on the part of the general public.

Each civilization operates in its living space or geographical landscape. An educational system has to train for mutual aid in the
conservation of the landscape which at the same time witnesses a
continuous struggle for existence. New technologies bring about
rapid and dynamic changes including explosions of urban growth
and the modern phenomenon of the supercity. A nation needs to
educate enough professionals—foresters, agronomists, geographers,

geologists, sociologists, and regional planners—to cope with the problems of space. The general public needs education concerning conservation and town and regional planning as aspects of mutual aid. No society can permit the pollution of its air and water or the destruction of its wilderness areas.[1] Accuracy requires an understanding of ecology as a struggle for existence in a natural landscape by competing entities. The impact of space travel has already transported humanity into new dimensions of philosophy, religion, technology and government. Our first steps into space have been felt deep within the world's psyche.

Time, the concept of temporal relationships, and—in the broadest sense—the idea of history is fundamental to any civilization. History is concerned with both the story of indigenous growth within a culture and external exchange or acculturation with other civilizations. Human history is the story of a vast acculturation—sometimes destructive, sometimes constructive. An educational system is generally required to provide students with exact knowledge of the narrative of civilization's movement through time. Without an historical perspective, the individual and the culture cannot have insight into problems of the present and without such insight there is little vision into the future. Nietzsche said that a sense of time or history gave "the capacity for divining quickly the order of the rank of the valuation according to which a people, a community or individual has lived." Estrangement from a sense of history may be a symbol of a nation's desperation.

Language, Art, Philosophy, and Religion

Language comprises paramount issues for education because it is the vehicle through which every civilization learns and grows, using its own linguistic arrangement of symbols. The clarity of communication (the logic and honesty of a message system) is vital to the existence of a culture. Equally as important is the freedom of experimentation in new and imaginative patterns of symbols in words, musical notes, mathematical, and scientific symbols. The restriction of language because of some limited ideology has led to destructive results. An educational system in the nuclear age must provide for

---

[1] Marston Bates, *The Forest and the Sea* (New York: Mentor Books, 1961), pp. 197ff.

adequate language teaching in the native and foreign tongues. Linguistics and allied fields can help clarify and control the message systems by which a civilization communicates. Language is also the imaginative exploration of old and new ideas. The realm of literature is the realm of imagination, and the writer may be the most dangerous and valuable man in the world because he uses symbols to evoke images that move the minds of men. Educational systems are concerned with fostering both accurate communication and imaginative literature.

Art is a vital factor in every culture. Even the most primitive peoples treasure art and design in their canoes, dwellings, rituals, and dances. In the realm of art, the polarity between aesthetics and utility is of primary significance. Bertrand Russell, in his *Education and the Good Life,* pointed out that every civilization must have a balance between utility and aesthetics. Great art has designed aesthetic forms out of functional needs. One of the major shifts in architectural history was marked by the construction of the Roman Pantheon. This building provided a new and also aesthetic solution of the enclosure space. The Pantheon was a huge concrete drum upon which a dome was imposed, creating a vast open space in contrast to the forest of columns involved in the preceding post and lintel method of construction. A crass utility can be very ugly. The Charing Cross Railway Bridge across the Thames River contrasts with other Thames bridges which are utilitarian and at the same time beautiful. A purely utilitarian culture is a dangerous pattern because it does not use the stimulation and balance which come from aesthetic values. An aesthetic flowering—whether it be in literature or architecture—is a good index to the vitality of a civilization and a period. The mid-twentieth century flowering of architecture with Wright, the Saarinens, Corbusier, Gropius, Mies van der Rohe, Niemeyer, and Stone is an example. A top-level educational system requires exploration of the arts by all students and provides insight into the theory of functional design which can bring a high level of engineering utility with pleasing form.

Philosophy creates and helps solve paramount issues in every civilization. Without metaphysics or a philosophical picture of the relationship between man and the universe, there is no civilization. Philosophy is concerned above all with value choices. One of the great antitheses in a value system for a civilization is the conflict between drives toward adventure and peace. Without adventure there is no survival, because the world is continually changing. Peace is just as necessary as adventure since man requires time for contemplation amid the security of a community of friends. Philosophy is vital to every individual, giving him a chance to visualize his own life style as well as the world picture in which he exists. Montaigne felt that the exploration of philosophy was usually delayed until it was too late and most mistakes had already been made. An insight into value systems is essential for education if it is to construct wise hypotheses for the future. Our modern world is one of the great periods of humanity and, like all great periods, it has elements of danger which require an alternation of peace and adventure in coping with the challenges brought by accelerating science and technology.

Religion, as an essential factor in every civilization, is concerned not only with ethics and the good life but also with faith and belief reinforced by a ritual and a communion of believers. In every culture a continuous struggle goes on to make religion relevant to the young and the old. In every epoch a nation has to face the challenge of providing varieties of religious experience which satisfy the individual's desire for an ethical life and for a faith in certain transcending ultimate values—a mystique in which he can believe. In the past, religion has been one of the great vehicles of civilization. Christianity, Islam, Judaism, and Buddhism have crossed the seas and continents of the world, bringing their cultures with them. Educational systems have experimented with various approaches to this issue, including state churches, "agreed syllabi," and separation of church and state.

Social Structure, Government, and Economics

In every civilization the relationship between elite and mass has been a challenge for the social structure. The old elites of the warrior and scribe have given place to the new elites of business, government bureaucracy, and military hierarchy. The elite systems are much more complicated than these terms suggest because to them must be added the great university and experimental centers and the centers of monetary and industrial power. If an educational system can produce an elite leadership which is an "aristocracy of talent" and a mass which is a highly-educated broad middle class, the culture has a good chance of survival and progress. The sociologists have carried out painstaking studies in social class and mobility which illuminate the relationship of elite and mass. An educational system is increasingly charged with the responsibility of training for excellence on many levels of talent and providing bridges at various stages of the educational process so that late-maturing individuals are not overlooked.

Education is faced with the problem of training for freedom and discipline in the realm of government. Some students of government doubt whether this can be accomplished at all. They insist that the state is basically amoral and imposes its controls on the individual in an increasingly pervasive totalitarian manner. The democracies of the world have demonstrated that education can train for a type of citizenship which combines individual freedom and self-imposed discipline. Government has expanded its bureaucracy with evidence of increasing concern about the welfare of the individual. Education keeps the channels of communication open in a democracy and makes certain that people use them. Educational systems train for a balance between freedom and discipline in various ways—the use of sports and games, intellectual rigor in studies, student government by prefects or school councils, and youth groups. The works of D. W. Brogan, James Pollock, and their colleagues in political science have analyzed many significant aspects of the relationships of government and educational systems.

The era of accelerating history in which we live has pointed up the challenge of economics to education. It has to balance the innovations and theoretical thinking on public defense, welfare, and education against the conservatism of holding the line on labor's level of income, capital resources, and a high level of luxury for the consumer. The United States in the mid-twentieth century constitutes a case study in the conflicts between private opulence and public austerity—*i.e.,* unbalanced expansion of private consumption and a lag in social overhead requirements in schools, hospitals, and public recreational facilities. The patterns of innovation and conservatism have changed from Adam Smith to Joseph Schumpeter, but the conflict continues and the educational system must cope with it. Cautious and modest improvement in educational strategy is dangerously inadequate in any country. As the Nigerian *Investment in Education* Report put it: "Nigerian education must for a time become an international enterprise. ... To entertain any more modest programme is to confess defeat." The writings of Theodore Schultz, Robert Solow, Gary Becker, J. K. Galbraith, Friedrich Edding, and W. W. Rostow are important linkages for the comparative education researcher in the economics of educational systems.

Technology, Science, Health, and Education

Technology is concerned with creativity in solutions but also must foster adaptation suitable to the individual culture. Technology needs to be investigated systematically in an educational system because it makes the web of life in which men live. Lewis Mumford's *Technics and Civilization* and Siegfried Geideon's *Mechanization Takes Command* describe the impact of changing technologies upon the texture of human society. Unless the public understands the array of instruments which it possesses and its possible consequences, it cannot make intelligent decisions. Automation, electronic computors, cybernetics, rocketry, space vehicles, power machines, and instruments have become dynamic influences which are being increasingly studied in basic courses. Adaptation is an integral part of any technological epoch in a culture's history. Transitions from coal to diesel locomotives have changed the pattern of transportation and the lives of the labor force. The creativity of the cybernetic, automation revolution in technology requires compensatory adaptations in the production pattern. Some implications for education are: less specialized vocational training and more generalized study of the sciences, mathematics, the social sciences, and the humanities.

Science should be defined, following Dilthey's suggestion, as an intellectual sphere in which the natural sciences and the human sciences work together. C. P. Snow's famous analysis, *Two Cultures and the Scientific Revolution,* depicts the crevasse which seems increasingly to divide the natural sciences from the literary and human sciences. The problem of the union of the natural sciences and the human sciences is a paramount issue because within these disciplines are developed the theories, the methods of inquiry, and the instruments through which all the major long-range factors are investigated and dealt with. Educational systems in Europe have emphasized a *studium generale* and *culture générale* in order to unify the study of all organized knowledge or science for youth.

Health has always influenced educational systems. The Spartans emphasized the training of the body, while the Athenians tried for a balance of both. The intellectual and the athlete have been contrasting symbols in school and college campuses, but the modern trend has been toward balancing intellect and physique. Terman's studies of genius indicated high correlation between levels of physical health and mental talent. The impacts of technology, urban living, and world conflict have heightened the health problems which face educational systems. A team attack by medicine, public health, psychology, sociology, engineering, and education has been underway in many countries.

Alfred North Whitehead wrote: "In every country the problem of the balance of the general and specialist education is under consideration. . . . At present our education combines a thorough study of a few abstractions, with a slighter study of a larger number of abstractions."[2] He later said: "What we should aim at producing is men who possess both culture and expert knowledge in some special direction."[3] The study of educational systems has shown that this concern about the relationship of specialization and generalization in education is fundamental in national policy. Civilizations need people who are both experts in their profession and who are knowledgeable and competent citizens. The controversy continues unabated over the best strategy of education to attain a wise balance between specialization and generalization.

The beginnings of our exploration of space in the second half of the twentieth century have underlined both the need to explore outer space as a cooperative human undertaking and at the same time to preserve and improve our own planet as the home of all mankind. Consequently we face a great challenge in international education—that of acculturation: the constructive and creative exchange of the elements in our various culture patterns. In the first century A.D., Quintus Aurelius Symmachus phrased the fundamental question which faces us in international education:

---

[2] A. N. Whitehead, *Science and the Modern World* (New York: The Macmillan Company, 1925), pp. 284-5.

[3] A. N. Whitehead, *The Aims of Education* (New York: The Macmillan Company, 1929), p. 1.

Why should we not live in peace and harmony? We look up at the same stars, we are fellow passengers on the same planet, and we dwell beneath the same sky. What matters it along which road each individual endeavors to find the ultimate truth? The riddle of existence is too great that there should be only one road leading to an answer.

The widening of our horizons through the growth of knowledge or science and the expansion of universal systems of education has given us our greatest opportunity to solve the paramount issues in the long-range factors of every culture.

The more than three billion human beings inhabiting our planet confront common long-range problems of survival and progress. One of the most hopeful trends in the century has been the formation of the United Nations and its specialized organizations including the Food and Agricultural Organization, the World Health Organization, and the United Nations Educational, Scientific, and Cultural Organization (UNESCO). The famous preamble of UNESCO proclaimed: "Since wars begin in the minds of men, it is in the minds of men that the defenses of peace must be constructed." UNESCO insisted that men must be permitted to pursue the ultimate truth and that they must have their media for the free exchange of ideas expanded. UNESCO fought for a diversity in human cultures based upon respect for all civilizations as over against the indoctrination toward a specific world picture through force and uniformity. The worldwide program of undertakings included the exchange of ideas on educational, scientific, and cultural advances through international meetings, publications, and exchanges of books and students, together with technical assistance for developing areas and fundamental education to combat illiteracy. In the beautifully designed UNESCO building on the south bank of the Seine River, seventy or more nations have worked cooperatively on the long-range problems which education must face. Eugene Black, in the first of his Stafford Little lectures at Princeton University, emphasized the need for common counsel, saying "there are good practical reasons why we should adhere to what he [Woodrow Wilson] called 'the great method of common counsel with regard to the common interests of mankind.' "[4]

---

[4] Eugene Black, "Ventures in World Order," *University* (Summer, 1962), 12.

Assumptive Worlds

Every civilization has an "assumptive world" which governs its objectives and operations. Hadley Cantril analyzed the concept in these words: "The only world we know is created in terms of and by means of our assumptions. It is the world which provides what constancy there is in our environment; the world which gives our experience its consistency. And it is a world of assumptions—a world which we could not have at all except for our past experience in acting for the purpose of enhancing the quality of life."[5]

Civilizations have always been in competition with each other, intent upon the survival and progress of their "assumptive worlds." Walter Lippmann has estimated the contemporary world situation as a competition between two civilizations and their strategies of education:

> It is often said that the struggle which divides the world is for the minds and the souls of men. That is true. As long as there exists a balance of power and of terror, neither side can impose its doctrine and its ideology upon the other. The struggle for the minds of men, moreover, is not, I believe going to be decided by propaganda. We are not going to convert our adversaries, and they are not going to convert us. The struggle, furthermore, is not going to be ended in any foreseeable time. At bottom it is a competition between two societies and it resembles more than any other thing in our historical experience the long centuries of conflict between Christendom and Islam. The modern competition between the two societies turns on their respective capacity to become powerful and rich, to become the leaders in science and technology, to see that their people are properly educated and able to operate such a society, to keep their people healthy, and to give them the happiness of knowing that they are able and free to work for their best hopes.[6]

The effectiveness of a national style in the world arena is conditioned by the excellence of its system of education within its own society and in its external relations. The developing areas in Asia, Africa, and South America want to mature and succeed by their own efforts. They want an educational sharing of science and tech-

[5] Hadley Cantril, *The Why of Man's Experience* (New York: The Macmillan Company, 1950), p. 35.
[6] Walter Lippmann, "Our Age, Radically New in Man's Experience," *The Texas Observer* (February 23, 1962), 5.

nology so that they may achieve self-reliance and dignity. These cultures will oppose the superimposition of another culture on theirs. There are as many roads to progress as there are countries. One great strength of a democratic national style is its respect for diversity within its borders and without. Diversity and mutual aid can help the world's civilizations to face the adventure of the future.

Bibliography

Ashby, Eric, *Technology and the Academics*. London: The Macmillan Company, 1958.

Bailyn, Bernard, *Education in the Forming of American Society*. Chapel Hill, N.C.: University of North Carolina Press, 1960.

Barzun, Jacques, *The Teacher in America*. New York: Doubleday & Company, Inc., 1944.

Bereday, G. Z. F., W. W. Brickman, and G. H. Read, eds., *The Changing Soviet School*. Boston: Houghton Mifflin Company, 1960.

Beeby, C. E., "UNESCO and the Reform of Education," *Yearbook of Education*. London: Evans, 1952.

Brogan, D. W., *France under the Republic*. New York: Harper & Row, Publishers, 1940.

Brubacher, John S., *A History of the Problems of Education*. New York: McGraw-Hill Book Co., Inc., 1947.

———, *Modern Philosophies of Education*, rev. ed. New York: McGraw-Hill Book Co., Inc., 1961.

Butts, R. Freeman, *Cultural History of Education*. New York: McGraw-Hill Book Co., Inc., 1946.

Caldwell, Oliver, "What Others are Doing?" *The Annals* (May, 1961).

Cantril, Hadley, *The Why of Man's Experience*. New York: The Macmillan Company, 1950.

Cassirer, Ernst, *An Essay on Man*. New Haven: Yale University Press, 1944.

Chase, Stuart, *Mexico, A Study of Two Americas*. New York: The Macmillan Company, 1933.

Comparative Education Review. New York: Comparative Education Society. (Quarterly).

Conant, James B., *The American High School Today*. New York: McGraw-Hill Book Co., Inc., 1959.

———, *The Citadel of Learning*. New Haven: Yale University Press, 1956.

———, *Kinder, Eltern, Schule, Staat*. Berlin: Cornelson Verlag, 1961.

Cramer, F. C. and G. S. Browne, *Contemporary Education*. New York: Harcourt, Brace & World, Inc., 1956.

Counts, George S., *The Challenge of Soviet Education*. New York: McGraw-Hill Book Co., Inc., 1957.

Cros, Louis, *L'explosion Scolaire*. Paris: CUIP, 1961.

Curti, Merle, *The Social Ideas of American Educators*. New York: Charles Scribner's Sons, 1935.

De Witt, N., *Soviet Professional Manpower*. Washington, D.C.: American Council on Education, 1955.

Diesel, Eugen, *Germany and the Germans*. New York: The Macmillan Company, 1931.

15–18 (Crowther Report). London: Central Advisory Council for Education, 1961.

Fitzgerald, C. P., *China, A Short Cultural History*. New York: Appleton-Century-Crofts, 1938.

Gal, Roger, *Histoire de l'Education*. Paris: Presses Universitaires, 1948.

Good, H. G., *A History of Western Education*. New York: The Macmillan Company, 1944.

Hall, Edward T., *The Silent Languages*. New York: Doubleday & Company, Inc., 1959.

Haring, Douglas G., *Blood on the Rising Sun*. Philadelphia: Macrae Smith Co., 1946.

Heath, Kathryn G., *Ministries of Education*. Washington, D.C.: USGPO, 1962.

Hitti, Philip K., *The Arabs: A Short History for Americans*. Princeton, N.J.: Princeton University Press, 1949.

Hans, Nicholas, *Comparative Education*. London: Routledge & Kegan Paul, 1949.

Herskovits, Melville, *Man and his Works*. New York: Alfred A. Knopf, Inc., 1948.

Highet, Gilbert, *The Art of Teaching*. New York: Alfred A. Knopf, Inc., 1950.

International Association of Universities, *The Staffing of Higher Education*. Paris: I.A.C., 1960.

International Yearbook of Education. Geneva and Paris: International Bureau of Education and UNESCO. (Annual Volumes).

Investment in Education. The Report of the Commission on Post-School Certificate and Higher Education in Nigeria. Lagos: Federal Government Printer, 1960.

Johnson, William H. E., *Russia's Educational Heritage*. Pittsburgh: Carnegie Press, 1950.

Kabir, Humayun, *Education in New India*. New York: Harper & Row, Publishers, 1955.

Kandel, I. L., *The New Era in Education*. Boston: Houghton Mifflin Company, 1955.

————, *Comparative Education*. Boston: Houghton Mifflin Company, 1933.

Kimble, George H. T., *Tropical Africa*, Vols. I & II. New York: Twentieth Century Fund, 1960.

King, Edmund J., *Other Schools and Ours*. New York: Holt, Rinehart & Winston, Inc., 1958.

Kneller, George F., *The Educational Philosophy of National Socialism*. New Haven: Yale University Press, 1941.

Knight, Edgar W., *Among the Danes*. Chapel Hill, N.C.: University of North Carolina Press, 1927.

Korol, A. G., *Soviet Education in Science and Technology*. Cambridge, Mass.: Massachusetts Institute of Technology, 1958.

Laski, Harold J., *The American Democracy*. New York: The Viking Press, 1948.

Lilge, Frederic, *The Abuse of Learning*. New York: The Macmillan Company, 1948.

Lin Yutang, *My Country and My People*. New York: The John Day Co., 1935.

Livingstone, Richard, *Education for a World Adrift*. Cambridge: Cambridge University Press, 1943.

Matthews, Roderic D. and Matta Akrawi, *Education in the Arab Countries of the Near East*. Washington, D.C.: American Council of Education, 1949.

McNair, H. F., ed., *China*. Berkeley, Calif.: University of California Press, 1946.

Mitchell, L. K., *India Without Fable*. New York: Alfred A. Knopf, Inc., 1942.

Moehlman, Arthur H. and J. Roucek, *Comparative Education*. New York: Holt, Rinehart & Winston, Inc., 1952.

Moraes and Stimson, *Introduction to India*. New York: Longmans, Green & Co., Inc., 1948.

Mumford, Lewis, *The Condition of Man*. New York: Harcourt, Brace & World, Inc., 1945.

Naik, J. P. and S. Nurullah, *History of Education in India*. Bombay: Macmillan, 1943.

Neff, Kenneth, *Education and the Development of Human Technology*. Washington, D.C.: USGPO, 1962.

Nunn, Percy, *Education, Its Data and First Principles*. London: Methuen, 1923.

Reischauer, Edwin O., *Japan, Past and Present*. New York: Alfred A. Knopf, Inc., 1946.

Riesman, David, *The Lonely Crowd*. New York: Doubleday & Company, Inc., 1953.

Rostow, W. W., *The United States in the World Arena*. New York: Harper & Row, Publishers, 1950.

————, *The Process of Economic Growth*. Oxford: Clarendon Press, 1952.

Russell, Bertrand, *A History of Western Philosophy*. New York: Simon & Schuster, Inc., 1945.

Sansom, George, *Japan, A Short Cultural History*. New York: Appleton-Century-Crofts, 1943.

Schneider, Friedrich, *Vergleichende Erziehungwissenschaft*. Heidelberg: Quelle and Meyer, 1961.

————, *Triebkräfte der Pädagogik der Völker*. Salzberg: Otto Müller Verlag, 1947.

Snow, C. P., *The Two Cultures and the Scientific Revolution*. London: Macmillan, 1959.

The Yearbook of Education. London and New York: Evans Brothers, Institute of Education, University of London, and Teachers College, Columbia University. (Annual Volume).

U.S. Office of Education. Monograph Series on International Education. Washington, D.C.: International Education Division.

Whitehead, Alfred North, *The Aims of Education*. New York: The Macmillan Company, 1929.

————, *Adventures of Ideas*. New York: The Macmillan Company, 1932.

————, *Science and the Modern World*. New York: The Macmillan Company, 1925.

Wissler, Clark, *Man and Culture*. New York: Thomas Y. Crowell & Sons, 1938.

Woody, Thomas, *New Minds, New Men*. New York: The Macmillan Company, 1932.

World Handbook of Educational Organization and Statistics. Paris: UNESCO, 1952.

World Survey of Education, Vols. I, II, III. Paris: UNESCO, 1955, 1958, 1961.

Yanaga, Chitoshi, *Japan Since Perry*. New York: McGraw-Hill Book Co., Inc., 1949.

Index